DEFEATING DOMESTIC VIOLENCE
IN THE AMERICAS: MEN'S WORK

ALSO BY LUKE DANIELS:

Pulling The Punches: Defeating Domestic Violence

DEFEATING DOMESTIC VIOLENCE IN THE AMERICAS: MEN'S WORK

Luke Daniels

*For Mike
in Bristol!

Luke
20/4/24*

H
HANSIB

First published in 2017
by Hansib Publications Limited
P.O. Box 226, Hertford, Hertfordshire
SG14 3WY, United Kingdom

info@hansibpublications.com
www.hansibpublications.com

ISBN 978-1-910553-84-8

A CIP catalogue record for this book
is available from the British Library

Production
Hansib Publications Limited

Printed in Great Britain

CONTENTS

∼ For Olga Daniels who birthed me and nurtured me ∼

ACKNOWLEDGEMENTS

Thanks to my dear niece Ava for putting up with my disruptions to her daily living as I struggled with the manuscript in sunny Guyana. Thanks to Cauline Brathwaite and Steve Cushion for reading and technical support on the document. Without the suggestions and expert editing of Margaret Busby this finished product may still be in the making. To all my children and grandchildren, apologies for all the missed meals and outings due, especially over the holidays. And thanks to my publisher Arif Ali for his patience over missed deadlines!

INTRODUCTION

Most people will have some experience of domestic violence at some point in their lives; how the experience is handled when that moment arrives could well determine if someone lives or dies. With one in three women abused globally it is likely everyone will know a relative, neighbour or friend who has been a victim of domestic violence. The aim of this book is to not only raise awareness about domestic violence but also provide some solutions to ending it. Defeating domestic violence will require men and women to be actively involved in the process. For far too long, domestic violence has been mainly regarded as a women's issue. To begin to address the imbalance, this book is especially aimed at men: fathers, brothers, uncles, cousins, friends, heads of government, men in government positions and in the social services, police men, judges, doctors and nurses, civilians – in reality all men, notwithstanding age or status.

Progress in ending the abuse of women is relatively slow because men have failed to take responsibility for ending it. If you are male and have never abused a woman, this book is for you. If you have abused women, it is directed at you. If you are American (meaning anyone born in the Caribbean, Central, South and North America), it is specifically for you. For too long the abuse of women has gone on with the majority of men who are not abusers remaining silent. It is time for the men who do not hurt women to stand up and say *No more*! Not in my name. It is time for those who have hurt women to get help to stop their abusive behaviour.

More than forty years after the United Nations made ending domestic violence a priority, the measures adopted so far have made little difference to the levels of domestic abuse experienced by women. Reducing the global figures for domestic violence requires nothing less than a world revolution in gender affairs. More radical measures than simply removing the woman from the situation and imprisoning the perpetrator have to be deployed, if we are to see any real progress in ending domestic violence.

Understanding the root causes of the abuse is essential in the fight to defeat domestic violence. Women the world over have long argued that two key elements of domestic violence are power and control. Some women cite inequality and patriarchy as the real culprit. Patriarchy is the source of abuse of women and it is impossible to end abuse if it is believed that patriarchy is something that existed somewhere in the distant past, or if it exists at all it is in some "third world" country somewhere. Patriarchy is often relegated to history because it has been able to transform and adapt itself over the centuries. Nevertheless there is a simple test to expose patriarchal rule-we need only ask who is in control of economic, social and political power.

Understanding the role patriarchy plays in domestic abuse is crucial in defeating it. In her book *The Creation of Patriarchy,* Gerda Lerner informs that patriarchy did not occur overnight but developed over a period of 2500 years, from about 3100 to 600BC.[1] The subordination of women was enshrined in laws with the formation of archaic states. Many of these discriminatory laws survive to this day. We need reminding it was only just over a hundred years ago that it was legal for a man to beat his wife in England, providing the stick he used was no thicker than his thumb, hence the "rule of thumb" as it is known in law today. The subordination of women is not inevitable; feminist anthropologists looking at the relationship of men and women, at different times and in different communities, have shown that it was more a relationship of "different but equal"[2] that prevailed in prehistoric communities. Some have linked the erosion of women's status with the rise of patriarchal rule, with its support for the abuse of women. With the establishment of the state, domestic violence was promoted and supported by the ruling elite-it was politically motivated action and it is only by political action that any real lasting change will likely come. Defeating domestic violence will entail defeating patriarchal rule. Although it is true that all men benefit from patriarchy, it is a tiny minority of men who are the real benefactors of this oppressive system. This group, nowadays described as the one-percenters, survive and prosper by their capacity to exploit the divisions inherent in our societies. Their main aim is economic exploitation of the masses of working people regardless of sex, age, religion, nation or race; it is in the interest of the majority of men to end this system of exploitation. The progressive government's focus on ending poverty in the Americas will help to undermine this group. There can be no end to oppression under a capitalist system bent on exploiting the majority at any cost. Motivated by greed, the rich continue to get richer as the "trickle down" that they promise is exposed as nothing but a myth, as evidenced by the poor continuing to get poorer the world over. Nowadays some Latin American countries are managing to buck the trend by lifting millions out of poverty with radical social programmes. We have a long way to go as Latin America is still home to 10 of the 15 most unequal countries in the world.[3] This economic inequality is recognised as one of the driving forces responsible for much of the violence in the region today.

Defeating domestic violence will require tackling a number of key oppressions that sustain the system of exploitation. It is a distraction to argue over a hierarchy of oppression; they are all finely intertwined and all have to be dismantled, if we are to see real lasting change in society. There can be no ending domestic violence without ending the oppression of women. The abuse and mistreatment of children often teaches them to accept abuse or to become perpetrators; there can be no ending of domestic violence while children are being abused. Failing to recognise the oppression of men will only prolong patriarchal rule. There can be no ending of domestic violence while men continue to be socialised to be violent in the interests of those benefiting financially from waging wars.

The focus here on ending violence in the Americas is a response to the rising figures for domestic violence and violent crime, including an increase of femicide in the region. According to the Head of United Nations Office on Drugs and Crime (UNODC): "Latin America is the region where guns are most frequently used to commit violent crimes" the head of the UN Firearms team added, "The mere fact that this region has the world's highest rate of shooting deaths is reason enough to take a serious view of the problem."[4]

A serious view indeed is needed, one that sees violence as a public health issue and uses public health measures to combat it. There is good example that this approach delivers results. Uganda, at one time with the highest rates of HIV in the world, was able to reduce the incidence massively by tackling it as a public health issue. With public acknowledgement of the pandemic at the highest level of government and a prevention strategy established "across governmental ministries and non-governmental organisations"... with "community mobilization for a grass roots offensive against HIV"[5] proving effective in halting the disease. This approach is needed to end violence in the Americas and arrest the pandemic of violence sweeping the region.

There can be no denying the magnitude of the problem faced, as, according to a recent study,[6] 41 of the top 50 most murderous cities in the world are located in Latin America, which boasts the seven top spots. Another report says: "Every 15 minutes a young Latin American – usually an adolescent male – is murdered... roughly 400 killings a day or 140,000 a year... what is worrying is the homicide rate is exceedingly high at a time when murder is declining virtually everywhere else". The region is home to just 8 per cent of the global population but records 37 per cent of the murders, with Brazil alone responsible for some 56, 000 a year, the world's highest absolute number of homicides. In 2015 Brazil recorded roughly as many homicides as combined deaths from conflicts in Afghanistan, Iraq and Syria that same year. "Even the world's hardest hit war zones can hardly compete. Between 2001 and 2014 roughly 26,000 civilians died as a result of the fighting in Afghanistan, over the same period 67,000 Hondurans were murdered. Honduras has one-third the population of Afghanistan."[7]

The violence costs the region dearly, amounting to an average of 3.5 per cent of the region's GDP, or $261 billion a year.[8] Recent studies in Britain put the cost for domestic violence at £5.5 billion annually;[9] while the financial cost of all violent crime for 2012 was £124 billion.[10] For the USA, violent crime cost $460 billion annually,[11] with the financial cost of domestic violence put at $5.8 billion annually.[12] The economic cost of violence and crime in Brazil was estimated at R$92 billion or 5.1 per cent of GDP in 2004. Governments have responsibility to put in place measures to stop this waste of precious financial resources. The cost in emotional and psychological pain is less easy to measure but no less important to end.

The focus here is in finding solutions to ending domestic violence in the Americas, and argues that this is only possible by pursuing measures to end all violence. The worldwide marginalisation of men in solving this social ill is partially responsible for the slow pace of progress in ending domestic violence. Men are the main perpetrators of violence and men must be seen as part of the solution to ending violence against women. The campaign in the West around the much publicised slogan of "Zero Tolerance" to violence is a good example of how Americans need do things differently. When used in the west, it usually is understood to mean Zero Tolerance for violence to women only. Zero tolerance to violence in the Americas must mean Zero Tolerance to all violence, including state violence. There are no "one size fits all" solutions to ending domestic violence and the measures suitable for the Americas will be different to those of other regions of the world, although there are many similarities.

Much of the homicide is by gunshot, because the region is awash with firearms, mainly manufactured in the United States of America. The "right to bear arms" of the US constitution, is literally killing us in the rest of the Americas, as the figures bear out, with the three countries ranked highest in the world for firearms homicides per 100,000 people being Honduras, El Salvador and Jamaica.[13] It will come as no surprise that the United States has the highest gun ownership rate in the world and the highest per capita rate of firearm-related murders of all developed countries.[14] One resident was recently arrested with nearly 5,000 guns in his possession,[15] and although this may be exceptional, it is indicative of the problem of the some 300 million weapons held by American citizens.

With the slaughter of some 89 people in the USA each day by firearm, it is disconcerting to hear an American president lamenting the fact that he is unable to rein in the National Rifle Association, as he led the nation in mourning the loss of nine black lives to a white supremacist attack on a church in Charleston.[16] What chance of tackling the mighty industrial military complex? The rest of the Americas must take responsibility for implementing measures to stem the tide of weapons washing up on our shores, or we will certainly suffer the dire consequences.

The problem is not only guns, as the "machismo culture" prevalent in the region, is responsible for the attitudes that make the violence possible; understanding how a macho culture evolved and is sustained will help with disrupting violent behaviour and stopping it. The history of the Americas is a bloody one, before the arrival of Columbus and much more so after. Patterns of behaviour are often passed down through generations and for millennia we have had violent patterns of behaviour passed down and now recognised as "machismo culture". Fortunately, culture is not something that is static but is continually evolving; it is imperative that this generation take the necessary steps to end the culture of violence being passed on to future generations.

Understanding how patriarchal rule instigated and sustains a culture of misogyny and violence is important in finding solutions to ending domestic violence. The belief that women are inferior runs deep in the region and Professor Ivan Van Sertima believes that myths have an important role in shaping the way we think and behave. There are many myths about male superiority in most cultures as a result of patriarchal rule. Van Sertima points to the African myth of Osiris and Isis and compares this with the later myth of Adam and Eve. "The woman in Africa was not seen as a rib or appendage or afterthought to man, but as a divine equal."[17] Gerda Lerner argues that the "symbolic devaluing of women in relation to the divine becomes one of the founding metaphors of Western civilisation". She goes on: "the other founding metaphor is supplied by Aristotelian philosophy, which assumes as a given that women are incomplete and damaged human beings of an entirely different order than men."[18]

The myths that support the notion that women are inferior to men must be challenged if we are to end violence to women. The myths that support the notion that men are naturally violent must also be continually challenged. Raising awareness of the way patriarchal myths has shaped our thinking and behaviour towards women for thousands of years will help defeat domestic violence. Men will begin the process of change when they understand how the system of patriarchy, not only pressured them into becoming fighting machines, but also coerced them into oppressing women.

Patriarchal rule is alive and well today, especially in religion, the military and economic institutions where it has been able to adapt and transform the way it operates. But we need only look at the facts of women's existence to recognise its influence today: paid less for the same work, having to fight for rights over control of their bodies, stereotyped as care givers and used as sexual objects, have little say in the running of government, suffer domestic violence, daily abused and mistreated in all manner of ways. A Gallop Survey has shown that Latin American women feel they are not treated with respect and dignity.[19] They are absolutely correct in holding this belief as the figures show that seven of the 10 countries with the highest femicide rates are located in the region.

Breaking away from patriarchal rule is not easy as it has shaped our lives for thousands of years, especially through the patriarchal family. Regarded as a building block of society, it not only "mirrors the order in the state and educates its children to follow it, it also creates and constantly reinforces that order".[20] The challenge is for parents to raise children in an atmosphere of love and respect without violence and equipped with the information to challenge oppression. Lerner reminds us:

> The system of patriarchy is a historic construct: it has a beginning; it will have an end. Its time seems to have nearly run its course – it no longer serves the needs of men and women and in its inextricable linkage to militarism, hierarchy and racism it threatens the very existence of life on earth.[21]

Men have been socialized by the state for thousands of years to abuse women and it will take more than legislation of a few years and longer prison sentences to change the culture of male violence to women. Working with perpetrators to change their attitude and behaviour towards women is part of the solution to ending domestic violence. Outlawing domestic violence is nothing but a fine gesture, if the support needed to vigorously implement the law and provide support for men to change is not forthcoming. Raising the awareness of those responsible for implementing the laws will be crucial for any success in defeating domestic violence.

It will take a cultural shift to end domestic violence. The scale of the problem is too huge for small underfunded, charitable organizations to make a significant difference. This is not to say those organizations efforts are not important, but they must be seen as part of a wider political action to end violence. Political action must come from government, as the human and financial resources needed will be significant. The changes will be revolutionary by western standards as neoliberal societies will be unable or unwilling to make the radical changes needed to end violence to women. It will mean at the very least many men in government giving up their seats to women-in short, starting the process of ending patriarchal rule. It is a start that Latin American and Caribbean countries met in Uruguay and approved the Montevideo strategy to Achieve Gender Equality in the region by 2030.

Because violence to women has been so deeply ingrained in society, defeating it seems like one of the hardest jobs and yet in some ways it is one of the easiest jobs, men will ever tackle, once they put their minds to it. The first step is for men to simply say NO! *No* to the abuse of women. Men are the main perpetrators and must take responsibility for their actions and the actions of other men. By making a decision to stand up to those who abuse women, men show that they care about the women in their lives – mothers, sisters, aunts, nieces, friends, colleagues and neighbours.

Many Latin American countries breaking free from neo-liberal policies are starting to put people and the environment before profits. The change in political outlook makes it more possible to adopt radical measures needed to end the violence in our communities. There is still a long way to go in achieving egalitarian societies; but the left-ward turn is taking Latin America in the right direction. It would be rash to assume victory will be straightforward, as neoliberal forces are not entirely defeated and are bound to resist change. It would also be naive to assume that men can overnight unlearn the sexist conditioning of a lifetime; but creating progressive political space can make a huge difference for change to take place.

Tackling the root cause of the problem is crucial in ending domestic violence. Several chapters here will focus on our history of violence, to raise awareness of where the culture of violence stems from. The history of our region is steeped in blood; if we do not critically examine this history we will struggle to find solutions to ending the violence. As well as looking at the socialisation for violence, attention will be directed at issues that impact on domestic violence such as sexism, racism and inequality. The scope of the book is as follows:

Chapter 1: Before Columbus addresses pre Columbian violence of the indigenous people and also examines the outstanding achievements of the civilisations of the region before invasion. Our true history is rarely taught in schools and it is important we have a complete picture of our region and its peoples and their achievements in the fight to end oppression.

Chapter 2: Discovery, Conquest and Colonization covers the violence unleashed by the arrival of Columbus and his conquistadores. The diseases brought and the horrific levels of genocidal violence of the Spanish conquistadores changed the social structure of the region forever.

Chapter 3: The Fight for American Independence looks at the struggle of the settlers for liberation from European control and its impact on perpetuating violence patterns in the region.

Chapter 4: Inter-American Wars raises awareness about the ongoing violence that carried over from the independence wars and helped shape the "macho culture".

Chapter 5: Legacy of Slavery and Native Genocide looks at the profound effect of the violence unleashed in the region and its impact especially on the indigenous and black communities.

Chapter 6: Civil War and its Legacy of Violence continues to severely affect the lives of most inhabitants of the region. It critically examines the emergence of the USA as an imperialist world power, and the consequences of its support for brutal dictatorial rule in the rest of the Americas.

Chapter 7: The Extent of Domestic Violence in the Region looks at the facts and figures for domestic violence in the region, so we have a clear idea of the challenges faced.

Chapter 8: The State's Response to Domestic Violence examines some of the government responses to domestic violence in the region, so lessons can be learnt.

Chapter 9: Government's Responsibility to End the Violence looks at solutions to ending the violence. It is only by a committed, concerted government response that the violence engulfing the region will be completely defeated.

Chapter 10: Defeating Domestic Violence – Men's Work will challenge men to take responsibility for ending domestic violence and will provide information to help men with this task. We will look at the "Stop" domestic violence programme for men. Men are good at making laws and although domestic violence laws are important tools, no amount of laws will stop domestic violence. Some laws can actually hinder progress, as exemplified by a report that the Ministry of Justice in England was "concerned that since harsher punishments for perpetrators were introduced, fewer women were reporting domestic violence".[22]

This is a political book and I make no apology for that. I have always argued that domestic violence is politically motivated violence in support of patriarchy. When men abuse and terrorise women in their homes and in the streets, it is action that supports a system whose aim is to subjugate women. In these times, ignorance must no longer be an excuse for domestic violence. Men must be made aware of the role their violence plays in the oppression of women.

The problem of male violence is region-wide and requires a joined-up approach to ending the conditions that promote violence, because the USA and Latin America seem to be moving in different political directions, I had considered excluding the USA from the scope of this book. But, like the proverbial elephant in the room, it soon became clear that the USA has too huge an influence in the region to be ignored. I believe that the solutions proposed here to ending the violence for the rest of the Americas will be problematic for an advanced capitalist society such as the USA, but some, like the "Occupy" and the "Every Life Matters" movements, have started to challenge and change the political discourse in the USA.

Having counselled hundreds of perpetrators of domestic violence over a five-year period at the Everyman Centre in London the author is convinced that deep down men are unhappy about the violence they do to women and want to and can change their behaviour. This book it is hoped will prove to be a useful resource for those in the Americas engaged in ending all violence and especially the violence done to women.

Notes to Introduction

1   Gerda Lerner, *The Creation of Patriarchy*, Oxford University Press, 1986, p. 8.
2   Lerner, *The Creation of Patriarchy*, p. 18.
3   United Nations Development Programme report, 2016.
4   Simonetta Grassi, UN Report 2015.
5   S. J. Genius, S. K. Genius, "HIV/Aids prevention in Uganda: why has it worked", Postgrad Med. J, 2005.
6   Mexican think tank: Council for Public Security and Criminal Justice, 2016.
7   Robert Muggah and Ilona Szabo de Carvalho, "Latin America's Murder Epidemic – how to stop the killing", Foreign Affairs, 22 March 2017.
8   Ibid.
9   Trust for London and the Henry Smith Charity report 2011.
10 Institute of Economics and Peace, April 2013.
11 2012 USA Peace Index, Institute for Economics and Peace.
12 2003 US Study by Centre for Disease Control and Prevention.
13 Bethan Owen, *The Washington Post*, 28 May 2014.
14 UNODC report, *The Washington Post*, 17 December 2012.
15 Reuters, "US-USA-gun", 4 December 2015.
16 Nedra Pickler, "Obama's 'N-Bomb' in racism podcast", *Metro*, 23 June 2015.
17 Ivan Van Sertima, *Black Women in Antiquity*, New Brunswick and London: Transaction Books, 1984, p. 8.
18 Lerner, *The Creation of Patriarchy*, p. 10.
19 Telesur, "Femicides in Latin America", 13 April 2017.
20 Lerner, *The Creation of Patriarchy*, p. 228.
21 Lerner, *The Creation of Patriarchy*, p. 229.
22 Andrew Sparrow, "Domestic Violence Laws 'backfire'", *The Guardian*, 14 April 2008.

Chapter 1

BEFORE COLUMBUS

The history of the Americas is one that is drenched in blood and it records some of the highest levels of violence in the world today. It is beyond the scope of this book and competence of the author to cover the history of all wars in the region, but in this and the next few chapters we will briefly examine some of that history of violence. It is important we are aware of this history of violence, in the search for solutions to ending the violence in the region today. It appears that the countries that suffered the most recent, brutal dictators are the ones that now record the highest murder rates in the world.

Studies have shown that violence is learned behaviour, often passed down through generations. As a result of the history of violence experienced by our ancestors it is easy to see how a "macho culture" could develop and permeate the region. Men would have been highly regarded and rewarded for their valour and fighting skill during the period of conquest, colonization, independence, regional and dictatorial wars. Now in relative peaceful times, fighting skills are no longer needed but still highly regarded and rewarded, as the socialization for violence continues unabated in the movies, violent video games and especially in boxing.

A brief history of the region is also useful in raising awareness about our origins and the struggles our ancestors faced. It is generally accepted that the first people to inhabit the "New World" (christened "America" by a German professor of geography who wrongly believed that Amerigo Vespucci was the discoverer)[1] were Mongols from Asia. They first arrived on the continent across the Bering Straits from Siberia, some forty thousand years ago as ice age primitives across an ice bridge. The bridge collapsed before reappearing about 25 thousand years ago, allowing for the migration of more Asians before its final disappearance.

The earliest inhabitants about whom anything is known are the Maya, arriving sometime between 2000BC and 1000BC. They occupied an area "embracing the modern region of Guatemala, Chiapas, British Honduras (now Belize), Yucatan, and the north-west corner of Honduras".[2] Some of the earliest human settlements found are in Guatemala, dating back to 6500 BC. It is believed that the Maya at Mirador Basin developed the first politically organized state in America around 1500 BC, named the Kan Kingdom in ancient texts. There were 26 cities, all connected by sacbeob (highways) that were several kilometres long, up to 40 meters wide, and two to four meters above the ground, paved with stucco.

Maya cities of the Peten Basin region, in the northern lowlands of Guatemala, had been abandoned by the year 1000AD. It is believed the Maya abandoned many of the cities of the central lowlands, or died in a drought-induced famine. Scientists debate the cause of the Classic-era (250–900 AD) Maya collapse, and many believe in the Drought Theory, because of ancient pollen and other tangible evidence discovered by physical scientists studying lake beds.

The Maya were a creative people who covered their buildings and monuments with fascinating signs called glyphs. They also wrote books known as codices, which they constructed by hammering fig tree bark thinly. These were then coated with lime and folded back-and-forth like an accordion, some stretching for more than 20-feet. However, much of Maya literature was destroyed during the Spanish invasion because the Spanish priests considered it "the devil's work." Bishop Landa, was the main culprit, destroying some 5000 Maya idols and burning every book he could find in 1562. Only a handful of artefacts have survived this shameful attempt to completely obliterate the Maya culture and civilisation. No one is sure, but it is believed that hundreds or thousands of volumes may have been burned, in the name of Christianity. Other texts rotted in the ground during the years before Maya culture was rediscovered. Very little is known about the civilisation of the Mayas, for the church and government officials went to extreme lengths to destroy what they saw as examples of "paganism". Fortunately, three books survived and are presently in European museums, thanks to patrons and friends of Spanish conquistadors in the 16th century.

Recently archaeologists have learned to read what the Mayas wrote, transforming the standard view of Maya culture. The Mayas recorded their past, the names of kings and queens and how they lived, and when they died. There are tales of artfully plotted wars, of battles and the capture of prisoners, of kings dying at their enemies' hands in ritual sacrifice. The reading of the codices have changed the belief that the Mayas were a peace-loving people, ruled by contemplative kings and astronomer-priests, to one of a collection of fiercely warring city-states.

The ancient Maya system of writing is hailed as one of the most remarkable achievements of the Pre-Columbian New World. The ability to keep information in relatively permanent records ensured continuity in the transmission of seasonal and astronomical data that could be passed on from generation to generation. This led to the refinement of mathematic systems and the development of a calendar far more accurate than that used by Europeans, well into the 16th century.

In his book *They Came Before Columbus* Professor Ivan Van Sertima argues that Africans came to the Continent in the Classic period and were responsible for writing, mathematics and astronomy developments. His study has cited the "African" heads discovered in Guatemala and he has given detailed analysis of the figures found. He argues that Africans had the ability, boats and skill to make the journey and has provided evidence in his book that they indeed did so on several occasions.[3]

It is believed the Arawakan-speaking Taíno moved into Hispaniola from the north-east region of what is now known as South America, displacing earlier inhabitants, they engaged in farming, fishing, hunting and gathering. In some areas indigenous Taíno, Arawak and Carib populations were continually at war.

The fierce Caribs drove the Taíno to the north-eastern Caribbean during much of the 15th century. There were two large empires in the region, let us take a brief look at them.

The Inca Empire

The Inca called their empire Tahuantinsuyu, or Land of the Four Quarters. Within its domain were rich coastal settlements, high mountain valleys, rain-drenched tropical forests and the driest of deserts. It is believed that the Inca controlled perhaps 10 million people, speaking a hundred different languages. It was the largest empire on earth at the time. Yet when Pizarro executed its last emperor, Atahualpa, the Inca Empire was only 50 years old.

The empire ranged 2,500 miles from Quito, Ecuador to beyond Santiago, Chile and was at its height when the Spanish arrived. The Coricancha, or Temple of Gold, boasted an ornamental garden where the clods of earth, maize plants complete with leaves and corn cobs, were fashioned from silver and gold. A flock of 20 golden llamas and their lambs grazed nearby watched over by solid gold shepherds. It is said Inca nobles strolled around on sandals with silver soles protecting their feet from the hard streets.

The society was highly organized and everyone was expected to contribute to the empire. Land was divided in three, with one-third worked for the emperor, one-third reserved for the gods, and one-third the people kept for themselves. All were required to pay taxes as tribute. The Inca had not developed writing but their tax collectors and bureaucrats kept track of things with quipu, knotted strings. Varying lengths, colours, knot-types, and positions, enabled them to store enormous quantities of information.

The Sacred City of Cuzco nestled in a mountain valley 10,000 feet above sea level, formed the centre of the Inca world. The first emperor, Pachacuti, transformed it from a modest village to a great city laid out in the shape of a puma. He built a temple and installed Inti, the Sun God, as the Incas' official patron. Some believe the Incas sudden rise to power could be down to the way Pachacuti expanded the cult of ancestor worship. When a ruler died, his son received all his earthly powers but none of his earthly possessions, which went to his panaqa, or other male relatives. The relatives used it to preserve his mummy and sustain his political influence. In this way dead emperors maintained a living presence. A new ruler had to create his own income by grabbing new lands, subduing more people, and expanding the Empire of the Sun. They expanded their agricultural lands by a self-help process, one couple helping another plant or harvest crops. They would in return receive help in their own fields. The Inca tailored this practice of reciprocity – give-and-take – to their own needs.

Their cities were centred on great plazas where they threw vast parties for neighbouring chiefs that could last for days and sometimes a month. Dignitaries were fed, and given gifts of gold, jewels and textiles. Then would the Inca make their requests for labour, to increase food production, to build irrigation schemes, to terrace hillsides, or to extend the limits of the empire.

Machu Picchu

The Inca were great builders, expert at working with stone and gold, they built temples and fortifications at Machu Picchu, constructed from vast, pillowy boulders, some weighing 100 tons or more. They carved a mystic column, the hitching post of the Sun from the living rock. Another slab nearby is shaped to echo the nearby mountain. Constructed without mortar, the joins between the stones are so tight as to deny a knife-blade entry. A vast labour force was required and there are records of 20 men working on a single stone, chipping away, hoisting and lowering, polishing it with sand, hour by hour for a whole year.

The Inca built a network of highways, one running down the spine of the Andes, another along the coast. Inca builders could cope with anything the treacherous terrain required, from steep paths cut along mountain sides, to rope suspension bridges thrown across steep ravines, or treacherous causeways traversing floodplains. Every mile and a half they built way stations as resting points. Bands of official runners raced between them covering 150 miles a day, this way messages could be sent 1200 miles from Cuzco to Quito in less than a week.

Despite its achievements the Inca Empire was a brittle one held together by promises and threats; it rapidly collapsed when

Pizarro executed the last emperor. Worship of the Children of the Sun was soon replaced under pressure from the Catholic priests with worship of the Christian god. The natives took what they had to from their new masters and held on to as many of their old ways as they could.

The Aztec civilisation

The Aztecs were the native people who dominated northern Mexico in the early 16th century. A nomadic culture, they eventually settled on several small islands in Lake Texcoco, where in 1325 they founded the town of Tenochtitlan. They called themselves "Mexica", from which the Republic of Mexico and its capital, Mexico City, derive their names. Fearless warriors and pragmatic builders, the Aztecs created an empire in the 15th century that was surpassed in size in the Americas only by that of the Incas in Peru. Population estimates vary, with one source putting it at two to four millions.[4]

Moctezuma I and Tlacaelel 1440–1469

Two primary architects of the Aztec empire were the half-brothers Tlacaelel and Moctezuma l, who began the expansion of the Aztec empire by waging a series of successful wars in conquest of their neighbours. At the start of Tlacaelel's tenure, the Mexica were vassals. By the end, they had become the Aztecs, rulers of a socially stratified and Expansionist Empire.

Tlacaelel rose to prominence during the war against the Tepanec in the late 1420s, and wielded power like a Grand Vizier until his death in 1487. He recast or strengthened the concept of the Aztecs as a chosen people and elevated the tribal god/hero Huitzilopochtli to the top of the pantheon of gods. In tandem with this, some believe Tlacaelel increased the prevalence of human sacrifice, particularly during a period of natural disasters that began in 1446.[5]

The reign of Moctezuma II Xocoyotzin

Moctezuma II was a notable warrior who extended the tributary system and consolidated the conquests made by his predecessors, as well as conquering new territories. His campaigns reached as far south as Tapachula in the Soconusco region and the Chontal Maya states of Xicallanco in Tabasco. Only the Aztec arch-enemies of Tlaxcala, Huexotzinco and the Tarascans, remained undefeated, as well as the Mixtec kingdoms of Tututepec and Yopitzinco, which did not interest the Aztecs. The Empire was at its height when the Spaniards arrived in 1519. Some sources claim that Moctezuma II and the Aztecs believed the arriving Spanish to be linked to the supposed return of an exiled god, Quetzalcoatl, who was supposed to return pale and bearded.

The Island Arawak

The "Island Arawak" were so called to distinguish them from their distant relatives the Arawak Indians, or Taíno, who still inhabit parts of the South American mainland. The Island Arawak mainly inhabited the Bahamas and the Islands of the Greater Antilles consisting of Cuba, Hispaniola, Jamaica and Puerto Rico. Despite separation by the Caribbean Sea they spoke the same language and shared a common culture. Little is known about their civilisation because they were quickly wiped out by the Europeans. This is how they were described:

> While not perfect, the Island Arawak's way of life was as near idyllic as any to be found outside the pages of the Bible or More's Utopia. And yet, within three generations of the Spaniards' arrival they are all dead; their civilization gone; their ever having been on earth no more than a beautiful memory lovingly evoked in this book.[6]

Anthropologists have speculated about the reasons for their peaceful civilisation and many believe that the climate and abundance of food led to a condition as close to paradise as one can find, "The Golden Age" as some have described it. They were a Neolithic or New Stone Age people who practised agriculture and made pottery. They spun and wove cotton and were the "original growers and smokers of tobacco".[7] They were skilled "canoe" makers and were "fond of singing and dancing and kept domestic pets such as parrots, flamingos and a very small breed of dog, now extinct, which had no bark".[8] They also played a form of ball game similar to the Mexicans and they had a pronounced lack of acquisitiveness or sense of personal property. As Peter Martyr wrote: "Myne and thyne (the seeds of all mischief) have no place with them."[9] We know a little of how they lived from the early journals of Columbus. For example:

16 October 1492 – "…I have no doubt that they sow and gather corn all the year round, as well as other things…Here the fish are so unlike ours that, it is wonderful…I saw neither sheep, nor goats, nor any other quadruped.."[10]

6 November 1492 – "met with many people on the road going home, men and women with a half-burnt reed in their hands, being the herbs they are accustomed to smoke.. They saw no quadrupeds except the dogs that do not bark. The land is very fertile and is cultivated with yams and several kinds of beans different from ours as well as corn. There were great quantities of cotton gathered, spun, and worked up."[11]

Sunday, 16 December 1492 – "They raise on these lands crops of yams, which are small branches, at the foot of which grow roots like carrots, which serve as bread. They powder and kneed them and make them into bread; then they plant the same branch in another part, which again sends out four or five of the same roots, which are very nutritious, with the taste of chestnuts. Here they have the largest the Admiral had seen in any part of the world, for he says they have the same plant in Guinea. At this place they were as thick as a man's leg. All the people were stout and lusty, not thin like the natives that had been seen before, and of a very pleasant manner, without religious belief."[12]

They were not the only peaceful civilisation in the region; other mainland North American Indians lived in peace until European intervention, as Aaronson notes in *The Social Animal*:

Changing social conditions within a given culture can lead to changes in aggressive behaviour. For example, the Iroquois

Indians lived in peace for hundreds of years as a hunting nation until in the seventeenth century a growing trade with the newly arrived Europeans brought the Iroquois into direct competition with the neighbouring Hurons over furs (to trade for manufactured goods). A series of wars developed and the Iroquois became ferocious and successful warriors, not because of uncontrollable aggressive instincts, but because a social change created a situation that increased competition.[13]

There is no telling how the indigenous civilisations in the region would have evolved had they not been invaded by Europeans; what is not in doubt, however, is that the European arrival spelt death and destruction for millions of indigenous peoples. That surviving indigenous communities continue to face oppression on a daily basis should focus minds in the region to remedy the situation. We owe at least this to the original inhabitants of the Americas.

Notes to Chapter 1

1 Eric Williams, *Documents of West Indian History 1492-1655*, PNM Publishing Co., 1963, No. 13 – Injustice to the Discoverer, p. 13.

2 D. A. G. Waddell, *British Honduras*, Oxford University Press, 1961.

3 Ivan Van Sertima, *They Came Before Columbus: The African Presence in Ancient America*, USA/Canada: Random House, 1976.

4 D. J. R. Walker, *Columbus and the Golden World of the Island Arawaks*, The Book Guild, 1992, p. 95.

5 Diego Durán, *History of the Indies of New Spain*, Norman, OK: University of Oklahoma Press, 1994.

6 Walker, *Columbus and the Golden World of the Island Arawaks*, book jacket.

7 Walker, *Columbus and the Golden World of the Island Arawaks*, p. 25.

8 Walker, *Columbus and the Golden World of the Island Arawaks*, p. 28.

9 Walker, *Columbus and the Golden World of the Island Arawaks*, p. 29.

10 Williams, *Documents of West Indian History*, p. 19.

11 Ibid.

12 Ibid.

13 Elliott Aronson, *The Social Animal* (6th edition), Freeman, 1992, p. 247, quoting G. T. Hunt (1940), *The Wars of the Iroquois*. Madison: University of Wisconsin Press.

Chapter 2

DISCOVERY, CONQUEST AND COLONIZATION

Understanding the social forces, customs and culture prevailing in Europe at the time Columbus set sail, will give us some insight into the mentality of the people who would come to occupy and colonize the New World. We have to go back to at least 15th century European society, which was in turmoil during "The Age of Enlightenment". When the notion that "all men were born free and equal" was stirring the vast majority of peasants, to free themselves from the tyranny of feudalism. Capitalism was emerging as the dominant social force and people were on the move in search of jobs and wealth, looking for new sources of trade and raw material. The Black Moors, who had occupied parts of Spain for generations would be defeated in 1492, the year that Christopher Columbus set sail in search for a westerly trade route to India and stumbled on the Islands, which he believed were "...those innumerable ones that are depicted on the maps of the world in the Far East...",[1] he named the islands the "West Indies", wrongly believing he was west of India. So who was this man credited with "discovering the New World"?

Born in Geneva of poor humble beginnings, Columbus became interested in astronomy and astrology after listening to the stories of seasoned adventurers. He was obsessed with the adventures of Marco Polo and the possibility of finding a new trade route to India became his burning ambition. At first he tried to persuade the Portuguese Royalty to fund his project but they were not impressed so he turned to the Catholic Monarchs, Isabella Queen of Castile and her husband Ferdinand, King of Aragon, who pursued a policy of jointly ruling their kingdoms, creating a Spanish monarchy. Although Castile and Aragon were ruled jointly by their respective monarchs, they remained separate kingdoms. After some persuasion the Royals eventually gave official approval for Columbus to make a voyage to reach India by sailing west. The funding for the trip provided by Queen Isabella.

Columbus set sail on 3 August 1492 from the sea port of Palos, Spain and on the 12 October landed on the island the natives called Guanahani, now known as Watling Island. As he took possession of the island for the Spanish Monarchs he marvelled at the beauty of his discovery. In his log book he wrote: "I can never tire my eyes in looking at such lovely vegetation, so different from ours... I found the smell of the trees and the flowers so delicious that it seemed the pleasantest thing in the world..."[2] It did not take him too long to remember the purpose of the mission he was on, as the very next day he recorded "I was attentive and took trouble to ascertain if there was gold.."[3]

Had the native people understood what he was saying when he planted the flag and laid claim to their island for the King and Queen of Spain the interlopers may never have made it back to their ships. If they could only peek into his journal and read that he noted "they should be good servants... they are good to be ordered about, to work and sow and do all that may be necessary",[4] it would surely have meant the end of Columbus and his men.

Unfortunately for the indigenous peoples, after travelling to other islands and founding the first New World settlement "La Navidad" on the island they named Hispaniola, he returned to Spain. On his return he impressed his patrons not only with stories of the riches to be had but of the "infinite number of souls"[5] to be brought into the Christian Church. His sponsors were suitably impressed and provided more ships and crews for his second voyage. This was a mission by Columbus to convert the natives to Christianity and enrich the coffers of Queen Isabella, in the process enriching himself and his conquistadors. The natives stood little chance and if the true story of the "pacification" of these lands had been told, there would be no celebration of Columbus Day in the Americas today – for this is a story of greed, betrayal, brutality and genocide. It is a story we must come to grips with for there to be peace, justice and progress in the region.

The journey has been a long and painful one. This is what Columbus wrote in his *Journal of the First Voyage*:

> They are a people so full of love and without greed that I assure your Highness that I believe there is no better race or better land in the world. They love their neighbours as themselves, and they have the softest and gentlest voices in the world, and they are always smiling.[6]

The same could not be said of Columbus and his conquistadors, they were here to get rich quick and at any cost. The very next day he observed: "I saw some of them had a small piece fastened in a hole they have in the nose and by signs was able to make out that to the south or going from the island to the south, there was a king who had great cups full, and who possessed a great quantity…"[7] Much of his log is filled with the concern for finding gold and spices and he prayed out loudly: "May our Lord favour me by his clemency that I may find this gold, I mean the mine of gold, which I hold to be here, many saying that they know it." He was not to be disappointed. On his third trip he wrote:

> To the gold and pearls the gate is already opened and they may surely expect a quantity of all precious stones and spices and a thousand other things….The opinion of all is that were all Castile to go there however inexpert a man might be, he would not get less than a castellano or two a day, and so it is up to the present time. It is true that he who has an Indian collects this amount…[8]

It was not long before Spain became one of the richest countries in the world and naturally wanted to keep the riches of the New World for themselves. Their Catholic rivals, the Portuguese, would not agree to any such notion so rather than risk war between the two Catholic Nations the Pope intervened and divided the New World between them. By the Treaty of Tordesillas, 7 June 1494, the Portuguese won from Spain the right to exercise sovereignty over all land discovered up to 370 leagues west of Cap Verde and the Azores. This imaginary line averted war and resulted in the approximate frontiers of Brazil being marked out, even before it was discovered by Pedro Alvares Cabral on 22 April 1500. The other European nations felt threatened by the new-found wealth, which made Spain a power to reckon with, and they sought to undermine this "Adam's Will" of the Pope as they saw it.

The scene was set for battles over the New World to last for centuries, when the King of France asserted in 1526: "The sun shines on me as well as on others. I should be very happy to see the clause in Adam's will which excluded me from my share when the world was being divided."[9]

The English had much earlier refused to recognise any division of the world when Henry, King of England wrote to Sebastian Cabot in 1497, giving permission "…to the heirs of them and every of them and their deputies, full and free authority, leave and power to sail to all parts, countries and seas of the East, of the West and of the North, under our banner and ensigns….to seek out discover, and find whatsoever isles, countries, regions or provinces of the heathen and infidels whatsoever they be and in what part of the world soever they be…"[10].

The Spanish made the early running and the conquistadores would lead the charge to "pacify" the region. In 1496 Columbus's brother Bartholomew founded Santo Domingo, Western Europe's first permanent settlement in the New World. By 1500 there were between 300 and 1000 Spanish settled in the area.

The Resistance

The local Taíno people, led by the female chief Anacaona of Xaragua and her ex-husband Chief Caonabo of Maguana, resisted this occupation, refusing to plant crops and abandoning their Spanish-occupied villages. However, within a few years of Spanish occupation the Taíno population declined drastically, due to oppression and diseases such as smallpox, measles and the common cold that arrived with the Europeans. Thousands of the island's Taíno were enslaved to work in gold mines. According to the best estimates there were 200,000-300,000 Taíno in 1492, by 1508 this figure was reduced to 60,000: in 1510 the number was 46,000, in 1512 it was 20,000; in 1514 it was down to 14,000, by 1548 it was doubted that 500 remained.[11] Such was the fate of those described by Columbus 80 years earlier as ''no better nor gentler people in the world''.

The Indians resisted in every way they could but continued to be murdered in large numbers: "They died, but they died with dignity and fortitude, these first colonial rebels against imperialism."[12] The story is told of Hatuey, who fled from Hispaniola to Cuba where he was eventually captured after they

threatened and tortured every Indian they captured alive so that they would confess where Hatuey was. They said they did not know...but finally they learnt where he was... and [he] was condemned to burned alive. When they were ready to burn him and he was tied to the stake a Franciscan friar urged him as best as he could, to die a Christian and be baptised. Hatuey enquired why he should be like the Christians, who were bad people. The priest answered: 'Because those who die Christians go to heaven where they eternally see God and rest' Hatuey then asked him if the Christians went to heaven; and the friar said that those who were good certainly went to heaven. Then the Indian ended by saying that he did not wish to go there, because the Christians were there... Thereupon they set fire to the wood and burned him.[13]

One of the good Christians was Bartolomé de las Casas, who campaigned against the enslavement and mistreatment of the Indians and reported to Emperor Charles V that he had seen with his own eyes "cruelties more atrocious and unnatural than any recorded of untutored and savage barbarians". This behaviour he put down to the

...greed and thirst for gold of our countrymen. They have been practised in two ways; first by wicked and unjust wars, in which numberless Indians, who had been living in perfect peace in their own homes, and without molesting anybody, were slaughtered. Their countries that formerly teemed with people and villages without number, have been made desolate; secondly by enslaving after doing away with their chiefs and rulers, the common people who they parcelled amongst themselves in Encomiendas of fifty or a hundred and cast them into the mines...[14]

The imperialist wars unleashed on the Native people were very one-sided. With superior weapons the Admiral

subdued by force of arms the entire island....for which purpose he selected 200 Spanish foot soldiers, 20 men from the cavalry, with many crossbows, muskets, lances and swords and another more terrible and frightful weapon against the Indians, besides the horses, was the 20 ferocious greyhounds which when released and told 'at him' in one hour tore each a hundred Indians to pieces; since the people of this island were used to go totally naked from head to foot one can easily judge what the ferocious greyhounds could do when excited and provoked by those who unleashed them on naked bodies of very delicate skins...[15]

With the mines exhausted, the Spaniards created a plantation economy on the island with Gonzalo de Velosa establishing the first sugar mill in 1516.[16] The colony for decades became the headquarters of Spanish power in the hemisphere and the springboard for the conquest of the rest of the Americas. The island of Hispaniola as we now know it was eventually divided into the French speaking Haiti and the Spanish speaking Dominican Republic.

Hispaniola quickly declined after Spain conquered the American mainland and most Spanish colonists left for the silver-mines of Mexico and Peru, while new immigrants from Spain by passed the island completely. Agriculture dwindled, new imports of slaves ceased, and white colonists, free blacks, and slaves alike lived in poverty, weakening the racial hierarchy and aiding intermixing, resulting in a population of predominantly mixed Spaniard, African, and Taíno descent. Except for the city of Santo Domingo, which managed to maintain some legal exports, Dominican ports were forced to rely on contraband trade, which, along with livestock, became the only source of livelihood for the island dwellers. English and French buccaneers gained a foothold in the north western coastal part of the island, and after years of struggles with the French. The Spanish ceded the western coast of the island to France by the 1697 Treaty of Ryswick, but held on to the Central Plateau. The French created a wealthy colony Saint-Domingue, while the Spanish colony suffered economic decline.

Conquest of the mainland
Nueva Cadiz was the first Spanish settlement on the mainland of South America – founded in 1500 on the island of Cubagua, Venezuela. However, the first permanent settlement to survive was Cumana in Venezuela. It was founded by Franciscan friars in 1501, but due to successful attacks by the indigenous people, it had to be re-founded several times, until Diego Hernandez de Serpa's foundation in 1569.

When Hernán Cortés landed at present-day Veracruz and founded the Spanish City there on 22 April 1519, it marked the beginning of 300 years of Spanish hegemony over the region. Cortés's conquest of the Aztec Empire (1519–21) followed by Francisco Pizarro's destruction in Peru of the Inca Empire in 1532 paved the way for the conquest of the Yucatan of Guatemala although this campaign against the Maya peoples in the Yucatan Peninsula of present-day Mexico and northern Central America lasted almost 170 years, from 1551 to 1697. A process that could have taken longer, were it not for three separate epidemics that took a heavy toll on the Maya population. It took nearly another 60 years of war (the Chichimeca wars) before the Spaniards could complete the conquest of Mesoamerica.

Fall of the Aztec Empire
The Aztecs were the Native American people who dominated northern Mexico during the reign of Huey Tlatoani Moctezuma II (Montezuma II) at the time of the Spanish conquest in the early 16th century. A nomadic culture, the Aztecs eventually settled on several small islands in Lake Texcoco.

The Spanish quickly used the often successful tactic of divide and rule when in 1521 Hernán Cortés, and an allied army of other Native Americans that far outnumbered the defending Aztecs, conquered them through germ warfare, siege warfare, modern warfare, and direct combat. The war was devastating for the native population:

> Central Mexico which had some 25 million inhabitants, was reduced it was estimated to a residual population of one million. The same 'abysmae' collapse occurred in the island of Hispaniola, in the Yucatan, in Central America and later in Colombia... This demographic collapse was quite unprecedented, out of all proportion even to the horrors of the Black Death in fourteenth century Europe.[17]

The states in the Guatemalan central highlands flourished until the arrival in 1525 of Pedro de Alvarado, second-in-command to Hernán Cortés. He was sent to the Guatemala highlands with 300 Spanish foot soldiers, 120 Spanish horsemen and several hundred Cholula and Tlaxcala auxiliaries.

Alvarado initially allied himself with the Cakchiquel nation to fight against their traditional rivals the K'iche'. The conquistador started his campaign by defeating the K'iche's 72,000 men, led by Tecun Uman (now Guatemala's national hero). Alvarado entered the K'iche' capital, and burnt it on 7 March 1524. He established his base in Tecpan, from where he made several campaigns to other cities and was named captain general in 1527. Having secured his position, Alvarado turned against his allies the Cakchiquel, confronting them in several battles until they were subdued in 1530. Battles with other tribes continued up to 1548, when the Q'eqchi' were defeated, leaving the Spanish in complete control of the region.

Conquest of the Inca Empire
The Inca Empire ranged 2,500 miles from Ecuador to southern Chile before the Spanish conquistadors destroyed it, taking advantage of a recent civil war between the factions of the two brothers Emperor Atahualpa and Huascar, and the enmity of indigenous nations

the Incas had subjugated, such as the Huancas, Chachapoyas and Canaris. A group of Spaniards under Francisco Pizarro deployed the same divide-and-rule tactic used by Hernán Cortés when, with the support of their indigenous Andean Indian auxiliaries, they ambushed and captured the Emperor Atahualpa and ransomed him for 24 tons of gold. After receiving the ransom from the Inca people, the conquistadors strangled Atahualpa anyway. This ruthless action of Pizarro should not surprise, as Fray Bernardino reported on his behaviour to Charles V, that "...he wanted to ship the Indians assigned to their service to be sold in Panama in return for wine, vinegar and oil... I told Pizarro that...the Indians should be brought to a knowledge of God and not be robbed and despoiled of their lands....Pizarro replied that he had come from Mexico to take their gold away from the Indians and that he would not do as I asked...he pleaded with me not to go and offered me my share of the gold..."[18]

The Battle of Cajamarca in 1532 was the first step in a long campaign that took decades of fighting to subdue the mightiest empire in the Americas. In the following years the conquistadors and indigenous allies extended control over the greater Andes region and the Vice Royalty of Peru was established in 1542.

After the indigenous people were defeated, the wholesale looting of the region began apace. The Spanish asserted their rule and justified their actions, as one Francisco de Toledo, Viceroy of Peru sought to reassure his King in 1573:

Your Majesty is the legitimate ruler of this Kingdom and the Inca are tyrannical usurpers...and as there are no legitimate heirs of the Inca tyrants, all the mines, minerals and agricultural wealth, all the idols and treasurers in the tombs, the lands and livestock reserved for the service of the Incas, and which are not private property, justly belong to Your Majesty as King and Lord as if it is property which was vacant, unowned and so to speak derelict.[19]

The early colonists
The first settlers left behind by Columbus on his first trip to the West Indies were wiped out and if their behaviour was anything like those Las Casas described, one could understand why:

...the Spaniards more and more forgot their origins and their arrogance, presumptuousness, luxury and contempt for these most humble people increased. When they got up though they had neither mules nor horses they would not walk any distance, but insisted on being borne on the shoulders of the unfortunate Indians if they were in a hurry or in litters slung in hammocks if they were not; and those that carried them taking turns, had to move swiftly. Accompanying the Spaniards were Indians who carried large leaves to shade them and others who carried goose wings to fan them...It was comical to see the presumption and vanity of the Spaniards how they esteemed and exalted themselves; those who could not afford a shirt of Castilian lined, cloak, coat or stockings, but wore only a cotton shirt...[20]

The Spanish at first tried to restrict entry into the New World:

"It is necessary to allow people from all parts of the world to come to this land to populate it freely, and to grant general permission for this purpose, excluding only Moors, Jews and reconciled persons, their children and grandchildren, as prescribed in the ordinance, since such persons are always evilly disposed, seditious and revolutionary in towns and communities."[21]

Capitalism's drive for profits promoted immigration to the region as King Ferdinand recognised that "the more people there are to work, the greater will be the profit"[22] and he joined with Queen Isabella to encouraged settlers in a 1495 decree "Any persons who wish to live and dwell in the said Hispaniola without pay, may go and will go freely, and there they will be free, and will pay no duty...may keep for themselves a third of the gold which they may find and get in the said Island, as long as it is not for exchange, and the remaining two thirds will be for Us..."[23] Later on the State aided immigration, and encouraged skilled trades men and the clergy "that the said number of three hundred and thirty persons who may go to the said Indies shall be paid and will be paid their salaries..."[24] Still more people were needed and it was opportunity to get rid of the less desirables, so yet another decree "that each and every male person and our many subjects and nationals who may have committed up to the day of publication of this decree any murders or any other crimes of whatever nature and quality they might be except heresy and lese majeste or…treason, or perfidy, or sure death, weather caused by fire or arrow, or counterfeiting, or sodomy, or stealing of copper, gold or silver…shall go and serve in Hispaniola at their own cost…those who deserve the death penalty will serve for two years and those who deserve a minor penalty than death, even though it might be the loss of a member, for a year and will be pardoned for whatever crimes and transgressions of whatever sort…"[25]

Other European nations would adopt the same policy to rid themselves of undesirables and the British would "send them for some of the new plantations all delinquents for matters which deserve not hanging, might be served too without sparing one of them …so should we not only free the streets and country of such rascals and vagrant people that swarm up and down at present":[26] the House of Lords was also petitioned to transport prisoners "to Barbadoes as many of them as the justices of the peace in the said country shall think fit to permit, so that this kingdom will be troubled by them no more, most of them being able young men and fit to do that country service…their crimes being but for petty things as afore said…"[27] why not get rid of political opponents too as Oliver Cromwell informs the Speaker of the Parliament of England "…two towers were surrounded, in one of which was about six or seven score…we knowing that hunger must compel them, set only good guards to secure them from running away, until their stomachs were come down…. they killed and wounded some of our men. When they submitted their officers were knocked on the head, and every tenth man of the soldiers killed and the rest shipped for Barbadoes. The soldiers in the other town were all spared as to their lives only, and shipped likewise to Barbadoes."[28]

Apart from the buccaneers and pirates wreaking periodic havoc in the region, Barbados was "inhabited with all sorts: With English, French, Dutch, Scots, Irish, Spaniards they being Jews; with Indians and miserable Negroes born to perpetual slavery they and their seed; these Negroes they do allow as many wives as they will have, some will have three or four, according as they find their body able…they cost them nothing the bringing up, they go always naked; some planters will have 30 more or less about 4 or 5 years old; they sell them from one to the other as we do sheep. This island is the dunghill whereon England doth cast forth its rubbish; rogues and whores and such like people are those which are generally brought here…a bawd brought over puts on a demure comportment, a whore if handsome makes a wife for some rich planter. But in plain the Island of itself is very delightful and pleasant…"[29]

Aesthetics apart, the beauty was in the extraction of wealth and the mercantile system was set up to facilitate this. The Spanish were successful with this system for a while before other European nations gained a foothold in the region and a more advanced form of capitalism set new standards for the exploitation of the region. The islands exhausted of their mineral wealth, would soon provide even more riches for the Europeans for another 300 years, with the production of "king sugar".

Demographic impact

The Indigenous peoples lived in North America for thousands of years, developing complex cultures before European colonists began arriving mostly from England after 1600. The European interlopers on the North American continent considered the Indigenous people primitive and sought to enforce capitalist-orientated values of civilisation on them. The indigenous people, for example, did not believe in owning land or property and lived communally; as a result much of their communal land was stolen from them and they were often forced unto barren reservations. Genocidal war would see an estimated five million Indians reduced to a mere 250,000 by the time the Wounded Knee Massacre took place four hundred years later.

Sherburne F. Cooke (1896–1974)studied the history of the indigenous population of California and from decades of research made estimates for the pre-contact population and the history of demographic decline during the Spanish and post-Spanish periods. According to Cook, the indigenous Californian population at first contact, in 1769, was about 310,000 and was reduced to 25,000 by 1910. The vast majority of the decline happened after the Spanish period, in the Mexican and US periods of Californian history (1821–1910), with the most dramatic collapse (200,000 to 25,000) occurring in the US period (1846–1910).

The Spanish colonies "maintained all the social distinctions prevalent in feudal Spain... The class structure was reflected in the grants of land. The working class plebeian, received a peonia a modest grant of land, together with gifts of wheat, corn and cattle. The noblemen the caballero, received a caballeria approximately thirty-three acres. The caballeria was equivalent to five peonias."[30]

Spanish colonies were usually rigidly stratified under a legal caste system, with peninsulares (officials born in Spain) at the top, the criollos of Spanish descent in the next level, followed by the mestizo population, then followed the descendants of the natives who had collaborated with the Spanish Conquest and at the bottom were the other native indios. The elites maintained the strictest discipline and control over the indigenous population with the Church, generally allied with the military.

Notes to Chapter 2

1   Williams, *Documents of West Indian History*, p. 7.
2   Williams, *Documents of West Indian History*, p. 5.
3   Williams, *Documents of West Indian History*, p. 15.
4   Williams, *Documents of West Indian History*, p. 31.
5   Williams, *From Columbus to Castro - The History of the Caribbean 1492-1969*, Deutsch, 1970, p. 20.5
6   Williams, *Documents of West Indian History*.
7   Williams, *Documents of West Indian History*, p. 14.
8   Williams, *Documents of West Indian History*, p. 18.
9   Williams, *Documents of West Indian History*, No. 189, p. 207.
10 Williams, *Documents of West Indian History,* No. 187, p. 206.
11 Williams, *From Columbus to Castro*, p. 33.
12 Williams, *Documents of West Indian History*, No. 87, p. 92.
13 Williams, *Documents of West Indian History*, No. 87, p. 93.
14 Williams, *Documents of West Indian History*, No. 91, p. 93.
15 Williams, *Documents of West Indian History*, No. 83, p. 88.
16 Williams, *Documents of West Indian History*, No. 23, p. 24.
17 J.H. Parry, Philip Sherlock and Anthony Maingot, *A Short History of the West Indies*, Macmillan Caribbean, 4th edition 1987, p. 24.
18 Williams, *Documents of West Indian History,* No. 120, "I Have Come to Take Their Gold", p. 136.
19 Williams, *Documents of West Indian History*, No. 117, p. 132.
20 Williams, *Documents of West Indian History*, No. 94, p. 99.
21 Williams, *Documents of West Indian History,* No. 39, p. 37.
22 Williams, *Documents of West Indian History,* No. 38, p. 37.
23 Williams, *Documents of West Indian History*, No. 34, p. 33.
24 Williams, *Documents of West Indian History*, No. 35, p. 33.
25 Williams, *Documents of West Indian History*, No. 36, p. 36.
26 Williams, *Documents of West Indian History*, No. 266, p. 288.
27 Williams, *Documents of West Indian History*, No. 267, p. 288.
28 Williams, *Documents of West Indian History*, No. 268, p. 289.
29 Williams, *Documents of West Indian History*, No. 270, p. 290.
30 Williams, *From Columbus to Castro*, p. 56.

Chapter 3

THE FIGHT FOR AMERICAN
INDEPENDENCE

As the colonies became more confident, better organized and more prosperous they were on a collision course with their European masters – leading to yet more violence. We will take a brief look at some of these wars as a way of raising awareness of our own and the struggles of our neighbouring countries in the region – as often these are not taught in our schools. We learn more about the colonizing European power histories than about the history that is relevant to our understanding of the region.

The colonists could not have been happy that they had borne the brunt of the struggles to subjugate the indigenous people and establish colonies only to hand over the spoils to a distant relative who regarded them as less important. Besides most of the settler population were now born in the Americas and had no particular allegiance to a King or Queen some distance away.

As the ideals of the Age of Enlightenment thinking with ideas of self-determination reached the Americas, the planters saw an opportunity to free themselves of the constraints of mainland Europe· and generally supported the French revolution. In French Haiti, where there were many educated mulattoes and freed slaves, the ideas of the French revolution spread like wild fire. It is not surprising that a French colony would be one of the first in the region to attempt to throw off the shackles of European domination, this following quickly on the heels of their mainland North American neighbours who established themselves as the United States of America in 1783.

The American War of Independence, or the Revolutionary War (1775–83) as it is sometimes referred to, was the rebellion of 13 of the North American colonies of Great Britain who declared themselves independent in 1776, as the United States of America. When France signed an alliance with the new nation in 1778, the conflict escalated into a world war between Britain and France, Spain and the Netherlands.

The war had its origins in the resistance of many European settlers in North America to taxes imposed by the British parliament. These patriot protests escalated with the destruction of a shipment of tea at the famous Boston Tea Party. The British government responded by closing the port of Boston and the patriots replied by setting up a shadow government. Twelve other colonies supported Massachusetts and they formed a "Continental Congress" that effectively seized power from the royal government. Massachusetts militia units and British regulars started fighting at Lexington and Concord in April 1775. The Continental Congress appointed General George Washington to take charge of militia units and he wasted no time in lifting the ban on black enlistment to bolster his army. Small all-black units were formed in Rhode Island and Massachusetts; another all-black unit came from Saint-Dominique with French colonial forces. At least 5,000 black soldiers fought for the Revolutionary cause. Slaves who were promised freedom for serving were betrayed and sent back to their masters in the south after the British forces in Boston were forced to evacuate in March 1776. The Continental Congress formally declared independence in July of the same year.

Britain was, however, determined to hold on to its colonies and war continued for another seven years until the Treaty of Paris in 1783, ended the war. By the treaty Britain recognized the sovereignty of the United States over the territory bounded roughly by what is now Canada to the north, Florida to the south, and the Mississippi River to the west. When Thomas Jefferson became president he purchased the Louisiana Territory from France, doubling the size of the United States. A second and last war with Britain was fought in 1812.

The casualties in the war were; Americans between 25,000 and 70,000 dead from all causes, with up to 50,000 casualties. France lost 10,000 mainly at sea. Spain 5,000. Great Britain lost

4,000 army killed in battle and 1,243 Navy killed at sea. Of the German mercenaries fighting with Britain 1,800 were killed.

The backdrop to the Latin American wars was The Napoleonic Peninsular War between France and Spain. The Spanish Monarchy was under a great deal of pressure and feared losing authority in the colonies so established assemblies called juntas in the Americas to rule in the name of Ferdinand VII of Spain. The Latin Americans had other ideas and The Libertadores (Spanish and Portuguese for "Liberators") seeing the uncertainty of Europe, and no doubt encouraged by the success of the American Revolution, seized the opportunity to fight for independence from Spain. The Libertadores were predominantly criollos (American-born people of European ancestry, mostly Spanish or Portuguese), bourgeois and influenced by liberalism and in some cases with military training in the mother country. They divided between those who were pro-Royalist and those who were pro-Republican, leading to internal conflicts in the colonies. At the time most authoritative positions were filled by the "peninsulares" (representatives of the Spanish monarchy, mostly born in Europe) with little sympathy for settler problems or interests. Although there was no legal distinction between criollos and peninsulares, most criollos thought that peninsulares had undue weight in political matters. These and other tensions would soon lead to a series of war in the region:

The Argentine War of Independence

Was fought by Argentine patriotic forces and royalist forces loyal to the Spanish crown from 1810 to 1818. The patriotic forces were led by Manuel Belgrano, Juan Jose Castelli and Jose de San Martin. On 9 July 1816, an assembly met in San Miguel de Tucuman and declared full independence, with provisions for a national constitution.

At the time Argentina was part of the Spanish Vice-royalty of the Rio de la Plata, with its capital city in Buenos Aries, seat of government of the Spanish viceroy. Modern Uruguay, Paraguay and Bolivia, which were also part of the vice-royalty, began their push for autonomy during the ensuing conflict and eventually became independent states.

The population of Buenos Aires was highly militarized during the British invasions of the Rio de la Plata, part of the Anglo-Spanish War. Buenos Aires was captured in 1806, and then liberated by Santiago de Liniers with forces from Montevideo. Fearing a counter-attack, all the population of Buenos Aires capable of bearing arms was arranged in military bodies, including slaves. A new British attack in 1807 captured Montevideo, but they were defeated in Buenos Aires.

The Bolivian war of independence

Began in 1809 with the establishment of government juntas in Sucre and La Paz, after the Chuquisaca Revolution and La Paz Revolution. These Juntas were defeated and the cities fell again under Spanish control. The May Revolution of 1810 ousted the viceroy in Buenos Aires, and established its own junta. Buenos Aires sent three military campaigns to Upper Peru, headed by Juan Jose Castelli, Manuel Belgrano and Jose Rondeau, but the royalists defeated each one. However, the conflict grew into a guerrilla war, the War of the Republiquetas, which weakened the royalist forces. Eventually Simon Bolivar and Antonio José de Sucre defeated the royalists in northern South America. Sucre led a campaign that finally defeated the royalists in Upper Peru and Bolivian independence was proclaimed on 6 August 1825.

The Brazilian War of Independence

Was waged between Brazil and Portugal. It lasted from February 1822, when the first skirmishes between militias took place, to November 1823, when the last Portuguese garrison surrendered. The war was fought on land and sea and involved both regular forces and civilian militia.

The Brazilian Libertadores created the Brazilian Army and Navy by forced enlistment of citizens and foreign immigrants. They enlisted slaves into militias and also freed slaves in order to enlist them in the army and the navy. Fights between militias broke out in the streets of the main coastal cities in 1822, and quickly spread inland, despite the arrival of reinforcements from Portugal. The Portuguese forces were able to stop the local militias in certain cities, including Salvador, Montevideo and Sao Luis. However, they failed to defeat the militias in most of the other cities and proved ineffective against the guerrillas in the rural areas of the country. By 1823, the Brazilian army had grown, replacing its early losses in terms of both personnel and supplies. The remaining Portuguese forces, already on the defensive, were rapidly running out of both manpower and supplies and were forced to restrict their sphere of action to the provincial capitals along the shore.

The war at sea was led by Thomas Cochrane, who experienced a number of early setbacks due to sabotage by several of the Portuguese-born men in the naval crews. But by 1823 the navy had been reformed and the Portuguese members were replaced by native Brazilians, freed slaves and Brazilian-born free men, as well as British and American mercenary forces. This helped to strengthen the Brazilian navy, which succeeded in clearing the coast of the Portuguese presence and isolating the remaining Portuguese land troops. By the end of 1823, the Brazilian naval forces had pursued the remaining Portuguese ships across the Atlantic nearly as far as the shores of Portugal. There is a shortage of reliable statistics about the war and the total number of casualties suffered by both sides remains uncertain with estimates ranging from 5,700 to 6,200 in total.

The Chilean War of Independence

Followed the usual pattern of conflict between pro-independence Chilean criollos seeking political and economic independence from Spain and royalist criollos supporting continued allegiance to the Captaincy General of Chile and membership of the Spanish Empire. What started as a political movement among elites against the colonial power, ended as full-fledged civil war.

At the time Chile was a relatively small and isolated part of the Spanish Empire, ruled by a governor appointed by the Spanish, who answered to the Viceroy in Buenos Aires. On 18 September 1810, Chile broke from Spanish rule, declaring independence. This declaration eventually led to more than a decade of violence that did not end until the last royalist stronghold fell in 1826.

Although the declaration of independence was officially issued by Chile on 12 February 1818 it was not formally recognized by Spain until 1844, when full diplomatic relations was established. In Chile September 18 is celebrated as Independence Day.

Cuba's war of Independence

After his second deportation to Spain in 1878, Jose Marti moved to the United States in 1881, where he mobilized the support of the Cuban exile community, especially in Ybor City (Tampa area) and Key West, Florida. He aimed for a revolution and independence from Spain, but also lobbied against the US annexation of Cuba, which some American and Cuban politicians desired. After deliberations with patriotic clubs across the United States, the Antilles and Latin America, "El Partido Revolucionario Cubano" (the Cuban Revolutionary Party) was officially proclaimed on 10 April 1892, with the purpose of gaining independence for both Cuba and Puerto Rico. Martí was elected Delegate, the highest party position. By the end of 1894, the basic conditions for launching the revolution were set, and on 25 March Martí presented the Proclamation of Montecristi, which outlined the policy for Cuba's war of independence:

- The war was to be waged by blacks and whites alike.
- Participation of all blacks was crucial for victory;
- Spaniards who did not object to the war effort should be spared,
- Private rural properties should not be damaged; and
- The revolution should bring new economic life to Cuba.

The insurrection began on 24 February 1895, with uprisings all across the island. Martí was killed shortly after his landing on 19 May 1895, at Dos Rios, but Máximo Gomez and Antonio Maceo fought on. The Spanish soldiers referred to the insurgents as "the men of Mamby" or "Mambies", named after the Negro Spanish officer, Juan Ethninius Mamby who joined the Dominican fight for independence in 1844. When Cuba's first war of independence broke out in 1868, some of the same soldiers were assigned to the island, importing what had, by then, become a derogatory Spanish slur. The Cuban revolutionaries adopted the name with pride.

General Valeriano Weyler reacted to the successes of the revolutionaries by introducing terror methods: periodic executions, mass exile, destruction of farms and crops. Weyler's methods reached their height on 21 October 1896, when he ordered all countryside residents and their livestock to gather in various fortified areas and towns occupied by his troops within eight days. Hundreds of thousands of people had to leave their homes, creating appalling and inhumane conditions in the crowded towns and cities. It is estimated that this measure caused the death of at least one-third of Cuba's rural population.

America entered the war when its ship the *Maine* exploded in Havana Harbour, killing two officers and 264 sailors. The attack was blamed on the Spanish and on 19 April, Congress passed joint resolutions supporting Cuban independence and disclaiming any intention to annex Cuba, demanded Spanish withdrawal, and authorized the president to use as much military force as he thought necessary to help Cuban patriots gain independence from Spain. War was declared on 20/21 April 1898. Spain sued for peace on 17 July 1898 and on 12 August, the United States and Spain signed a protocol of Peace, in which Spain agreed to relinquish all claim of sovereignty and title over Cuba. On December 10, 1898, the United States and Spain signed the Treaty of Paris, recognizing Cuban independence.

The Dominican Independence War
Gave the Dominican Republic autonomy from Haiti on 27 February 1844. Before the war, the island of Hispaniola had been united under the Haitian government for a period of 22 years when the newly independent nation merged with Haiti in 1822. Previously known as the Captaincy General of Santo Domingo, the "criollo" class within the country overthrew the Spanish crown in 1821 before unifying with Haiti a year later.

At the time Haiti had been economically and militarily powerful and had a population 8 to 10 times larger than the former Spanish colony. The Dominican military officers were attracted to Haiti's perceived wealth and power at the time and agreed to merge the newly independent nation with Haiti, as they sought political stability under the Haitian president Jean-Pierre Boyer. However, due to the Haitian government's mismanagement, heavy taxes, military disputes, and an economic crisis the Haitian government became increasingly unpopular and a resistance movement called La Trinitaria ("The Trinity") was founded in 1838 under Juan Pablo Duarte, an educated nationalist. The Dominican resistance movement eventually ousted the Haitian occupying force from the country, and successfully resisted a series of failed Haitian incursions before declaring independence on 27 February 1844.

Guatemala War of Independence

Guatemala was part of the Captaincy General of Guatemala, for nearly 300 years; this Captaincy, or Capitana, comprised the territories of Chiapas, Campeche, Tabasco in modern Mexico, and the modern countries of Guatemala, El Salvador, Honduras, Nicaragua and Costa Rica. The Capitana gained independence from Spain on 15 September 1821 but this was shortlived, as the conservative leaders in Guatemala welcomed annexation by the First Mexican Empire of Agustín de Iturbide on 5 January 1822, and became a part of the First Mexican Empire until 1823.

From 1824 it was a part of the Federal Republic of Central America which had on 1 July 1823, declared absolute independence from Spain, Mexico, and any other foreign nation, including North America and a Republican system of government was established. For a period it belonged to a federation called the United Provinces of Central America, which broke up in civil war in 1838–40 and dissolved in 1841 when Guatemala became fully independent.

Guatemala's Caudillo Rafael Carrera was instrumental in leading the revolt against the federal government and breaking apart the United Provinces. Carrera relied on Belgium for support and in 1843 the Guatemalan parliament authorized the Compagnie belge de colonisation (Belgian Colonization Company), commissioned by Belgian King Leopold l, as the administrator of Santo Tomas, Guatemala. Belgium continued to administer Santo Tomas until 1854, when it withdrew because of financial issues and personnel losses due to endemic diseases such as yellow fever and malaria.

Carrera became leader with the backing of a coalition of conservatives, large land owners and the Catholic Church from 1844 to 1848, and then from 1851 to his death in 1865. Guatemala's "Liberal Revolution" came in 1871 under the leadership of Justo Rufino Barrios, who sought to modernize the country, improve trade, and introduce new crops and manufacturing. During this era, coffee became an important export crop for Guatemala. Barrios had ambitions of reuniting Central America, and took the country to war in an unsuccessful attempt to attain this. He died on the battlefield in 1885 against forces in El Salvador.

The Haitian Revolution (1791–1804)

Was preceded by, and no doubt influenced by the North American and French Revolutions but it was independent of them. The Age of Enlightenment Thinking appealed to the Haitian masses as much as to the French peasants. The planter class in Haiti also supported the revolution as they saw an opportunity to free themselves from the constraints of France. The freemen and mulattoes also supported the revolution, but for different reasons, as they saw an opportunity for equality and justice. The enslaved Africans could see no benefits for themselves and were against the planters seizing power as they felt they would be treated even worse, without the restraining hand of the French government.

With turmoil in France and conflict in the colony, the slaves under the leadership of Toussaint L'Ouverture, a former slave, seized the opportunity and organized an effective guerrilla war against the island's colonial population. Toussaint found able generals in two other former slaves, Dessalines and Henri Christophe who were able to defeat the planters. Toussaint became governor-general of the colony and in 1801 liberated the Spanish portion of the island, freeing the slaves there. Toussaint made peace with revolutionary France after they abolished slavery in 1795 but he was later betrayed and died in a French jail. The Haitian Revolution was the only slave revolt that led to the founding of a state; and it is considered the most successful slave rebellion ever to have occurred.

The revolt that began in April of 1791 ended in November of 1803 when the French were defeated at the Battle of Vertieres. It has been estimated that the slave rebellion resulted in the death of 350,000 Haitians and 50,000 European troops. Two months after defeating Napoleon Bonaparte's colonial forces, Jean-Jacques Dessalines proclaimed the independence of Saint-Domingue, renaming the country Haiti after its original Arawak name on 1 January 1804.

In 1804, from early February until 22 April, a massacre was carried out against the remaining white population of French Creoles in Haiti by the black population on the orders of Dessalines. Across the territory of Haiti, mass killings, plunder and rape took place on the streets and on places outside the cities, with women and children generally killed last. Some 3,000 to 5,000 people were killed and the white Haitians were practically eradicated.

The Mexican War of Independence
Between the criollos and European Spanish ended the rule of Spain in the territory of New Spain.

It is argued that the struggle for Mexican independence began in the decades after the Spanish conquest of the Aztec Empire, when Martin Cortés (son of Hernán Cortés and La Malinche) led a revolt against the Spanish colonial government in order to eliminate privileges for the conquistadors. This quest for Mexican independence from Spanish rule was also ignited by the ideas of the Enlightenment movement sweeping Europe and by the French Revolution and no doubt bolstered by the independence movements in the region.

Unlike some of the other independence struggles Crillos and peninsulares came together in Mexico to shake of the shackles of Spain. They agreed a number of principles including that criollos and peninsulares would enjoy equal rights and privileges, and that the Roman Catholic Church would retain its privileges and position as the official religion of the land. After convincing his troops to accept the principles, which were promulgated on 24 February 1821, as the Plan of Iguala, Iturbide persuaded Guerrero to join his forces in support of the new conservative manifestation of the independence movement. A new army, the Army of the Three Guarantees, was joined by rebel forces from all over Mexico and was placed under Iturbide's command to enforce the Plan of Iguala.

With defeat staring him in the face, the Viceroy resigned and on 24 August 1821 representatives of the Spanish crown and Iturbide signed the Treaty of Cordoba. The treaty recognized Mexican independence under the terms of the Plan of Iguala. On 27 September, the Army of the Three Guarantees entered Mexico City and the following day Iturbide proclaimed the independence of the Mexican Empire, as New Spain was to be now called.

The Peruvian War of Independence

Was a series of military conflicts beginning in 1811 and culminating in proclamation of independence by Jose de San Martin on 28 July 1821. The wars of independence took place with the 1780-81 uprising by indigenous leader Tupac Amaru ll in mind. During the previous decade Peru had been a stronghold for royalists, who fought those in favour of independence in Upper Peru.

After the war the liberators attempted to decide the political fate of Peru with San Martín opting for a Constitutional Monarchy, while Simon Bolivar (Head of the Northern Expedition) opted for a Republican government, both agreed it must be independent of Spain. On 22 September 1822 General San Martin abandoned Peru and left command of the Independence movement to Simón Bolivar.

After the declaration of Independence, the Peruvian state was bogged down by civil war. The republicans controlled the coast and northern Peru, while the rest of the country was under the control of Viceroy La Serna, who had established his capital in the city of Cuzco. Following the self-exile of San Martin, and the constant military defeats under President Jose de la Riva Aguero, congress requested the help of Simón Bolívar, who arrived in Lima on 10 December 1823.

An uprising in the royalist camp in Alto Peru (modern Bolivia) in 1824 paved the way for the battles of Junin and Ayacucho. The Peruvian Army triumphed in the battle of Junin under the command of Simón Bolivar, and in the battle of Ayacucho under the command of General Antonio José de Sucre. The end of the battle led to the end of colonialism in Latin America but the war continued until the last royalist surrendered the Real Felipe Fortress in 1826.

Uruguay's war of independence

Little is known of the Charrua who inhabited what is now Uruguay but ancient rock art, has been found at several locations. The Portuguese first explored the region in 1512-13 before the Spanish arrived in 1516. There was limited settlement in the region during the 16th and 17th centuries due to fierce resistance to conquest by the Charrua, combined with the absence of gold and silver. When Uruguay became a contested zone between the Spanish and Portuguese empires José Gervasio Artigas launched a successful revolt against Spain, defeating them on 18 May 1811 in the Battle of Las Piedras. In 1814 he formed the Liga Federal (Federal League), of which he was declared Protector and subsequently became Uruguay's national hero.

In August 1816 forces from Brazil invaded the Eastern Province and occupied Montevideo on 20 January 1817. They finally defeated Artigas in the Battle of Tacuarembó after three years of fighting in the countryside. In 1821, Brazil annexed the Eastern Province of the Rio de la Plata (present-day Uruguay), under the name of Provincia Cisplatina.

This led to the 500-day Cisplatine War in which neither side gained the upper hand, and the Treaty of Montevideo, fostered by Britain in 1828, gave birth to Uruguay as an independent state. The nation's first constitution was adopted on 18 July 1830. For the remainder of the 19th century Uruguay would experience a series of conflicts with neighbouring states.

The Venezuelan War of Independence (1811–1823)

Was waged against rule by the Spanish Empire. On 5 July 1811, seven of the 10 provinces of the Captaincy general of Venezuela declared their independence. The First Republic of Venezuela was lost in 1812 following the 1812 Caracas earthquake and the Battle of La Victoria. However, Simon Bolivar led an "Admirable Campaign" to retake Venezuela, establishing the

Second Republic of Venezuela in 1813; but this too did not last, falling to a combination of a local uprising and Spanish royalist re-conquest. Only as part of Bolivar's campaign to liberate New Granada in 1819-20 did Venezuela achieve a lasting independence from Spain (initially as part of Gran Colombia).

On 17 December 1819 the Congress of Angostura declared Gran Colombia an independent country. After two more years of war, which, it is claimed, killed half of Venezuela's Caucasian population, the country achieved independence from Spain in 1821 under the leadership of Simon Bolivar. Venezuela, along with the present-day countries of Colombia, Panama, and Ecuador, formed part of the Republic of Gran Colombia until 1830, when Venezuela separated and became a sovereign country.

Chapter 4

INTER-AMERICAN WARS

After the independence wars from European control the newly independent states would soon become embroiled in inter-regional wars, leaving feelings of hostility and mistrust for generations. The huge problem with violence in the region, including domestic violence, is a result of the socialization for violence that is absolutely necessary in the execution of war. A commitment to peaceful co-existence will reduce the need for preparation for war and free up the resources needed to improve the economic well-being of the vast majority, especially in the areas of health and education, which are often badly lacking. We will now take a brief look at some of the regional wars that have contributed to the culture of violence in the region.

Argentina and Brazil (1825-28)

The Cisplatine War grew out of the latent colonial rivalry between Spain and Portugal over control of the Banda Oriental, territory comprising present-day Uruguay. In early 1817 Portuguese forces seized the area after the defeat of the army led by Uruguay's independence leader José Gervasio Artigas. Relations between Argentina and Brazil had been tense for years and deteriorated rapidly after 1824, when bilateral negotiations for the creation of an independent Uruguayan nation were broken off.

When a group of Uruguayan patriots, the Thirty-Three Immortals (also sometimes referred to as the Thirty-Three Easterners, or Orientals), invaded the Banda Oriental from Argentine territory in April 1825, it sparked an insurgent movement that gained the support of several thousand fighters. Brazil accused Argentina of providing material support for the invasion and by May 1825 war seemed imminent, despite the Argentine government having no standing army or naval force. Both these military bodies had disintegrated during the years of civil war following independence. A new national army was quickly organized, with each of the nation's nine provinces called upon to send a complement of soldiers proportionate to the size of its population.

On the eve of battle a naval squadron commanded by the Irish-born Admiral Guillermo Brown was organized. Supreme command over both forces rested with Argentina's first national president, Bernardino Rivadavia. In December 1825 Brazil declared war on Argentina for allegedly having broken its neutrality by aiding the Uruguayan patriots, a claim denied by the Argentine government. During the first year of the conflict, most of the battles occurred at sea, as the small, poorly equipped Argentine navy sought to break Brazil's blockade of its Buenos Aires port. The conflict lasted nearly three years until a mediated settlement resulted in the creation of Uruguay, as an independent buffer state, between the two rival powers. Under the terms of peace agreed to in mid-1828, both countries were to withdraw their military forces over a two-month period and pledged to guarantee Uruguay's independence for the next five years.

The War of the Confederation (1836–39)

Was a conflict between the Peru-Bolivian Confederation on one side and Chile, Peruvian dissidents and Argentina, on the other. The war was precipitated by the creation of the Peru-Bolivian Confederation by Marshal Andres de Santa Cruz in 1836. The potential power of this confederation aroused the opposition of Argentina and, above all, Chile, due not only to its great territorial expanse but also to the perceived threat that such a rich state signified for the area.

Concern that the new Confederacy would break the regional balance of power and could even be a threat to Chilean independence, was just one of the reasons behind the war. On another level, both countries were in heated competition for control of the commercial routes on the Pacific; added to this the Chileans already had a strained relationship with independent Peru because of economic rivalry between their ports of Callo and Valparaiso. The North-Peruvian landowners also viewed the Confederacy as a most serious threat to their economic interests. The war was fought mostly in the actual territory of Peru and ended with a Confederate defeat and dissolution of the Confederacy.

The Platine War (18 August 1851– 3 February 1852)

Was fought between the Argentine Confederation and an alliance consisting of the Empire of Brazil, Uruguay, and the Argentine provinces of Entre Rios and Corrientes. The war was part of a long-running contest between Argentina and Brazil for influence over Uruguay and Paraguay, and hegemony over the Platine region (areas bordering the Río de la Plata). The conflict took place in Uruguay, on the Río de la Plata, and north-eastern Argentina.

In 1850, the Platine region was politically unstable and the Governor of Buenos Aires, Juan Manuel de Rosas, used his position to gain dictatorial control over other Argentine provinces. His rule was, however, plagued by a series of regional rebellions, including in Uruguay, which struggled with a long-running civil war, started after independence from Brazil in 1828. Rosas backed the Uruguayan Blanco party in this conflict, and wanted to extend Argentine borders to areas formerly occupied by the Spanish Vice-royalty of the Río de la Plata. This meant asserting control over Uruguay, Paraguay, and Bolivia. His objective also threatened Brazilian interests and sovereignty, since the old Spanish Vice-royalty had included territories that had since been assimilated into Brazil's province of Rio Grande do Sul.

Brazil actively pursued ways to resist Rosa and in 1851, it allied with the Argentine breakaway provinces of Corrientes and Entre Rios and also joined with the anti-Rosas faction in Uruguay. Brazil next secured the south-western flank by signing defensive alliances with Paraguay and Bolivia. Faced with an offensive alliance against his regime, Rosa declared war on Brazil. Allied forces then advanced into Uruguayan territory, defeating the Rosa's-aligned faction led by Manuel Oribe.

The War ended in 1852 with the allied victory at the Battle of Caseros, establishing Brazilian hegemony over much of South America. However, the end of the war did not completely resolve all issues within the Platine region. Conflict continued in the following years, with internal disputes among political factions in Uruguay, a long civil war in Argentina, and an emergent Paraguay asserting its claims. During the next two decades, two more major international wars followed, as a result of territorial ambitions and conflicts over influence.

The Paraguayan War

Also known as the War of the Triple Alliance (Spanish: Guerra de la Triple Alianza; Portuguese: Guerra da Tríplice Aliança), and in Paraguay as the "Great War", was an international military conflict in South America from 1864 to 1870 between Paraguay and the Triple Alliance of Argentina, Brazil and Uruguay.

This war, the most destructive in modern times in the region, has been attributed to the after-effects of colonialism in South America. The struggle for physical power among neighbouring nations over the strategic Rio de la Plata region, Brazilian and Argentine meddling in internal Uruguayan politics, Solano López's efforts to help allies in Uruguay and his presumed expansionist ambitions are held partially responsible for the war. Paraguay also had recurring boundary disputes and tariff issues with Argentina and Brazil for many years; its aid to allies in Uruguay in the period before the war worsened its relations with those countries.

After the Triple Alliance defeated Paraguay in conventional warfare, its people conducted a drawn-out guerrilla-style resistance that resulted in the destruction of the Paraguayan military and much of the civilian population. The guerrilla war lasted until López was killed by Brazilian forces on 1 March 1870. Towards the end of the war and with Paraguay suffering severe shortages of weapons and supplies, López reacted with draconian attempts to keep order, ordering troops to kill any combatant, including officers, who talked of surrender. As a result, paranoia prevailed in the army, and soldiers fought to the bitter end in a resistance movement that resulted in more destruction in the country.

The war caused approximately 400,000 deaths, one of the highest ratios of fatalities to combatants of any war in South American modern history. One estimate places total Paraguayan losses through both war and disease as high as 1.2million people, or 90 per cent of its pre-war population. The specific numbers of casualties are hotly disputed. Accurate casualty numbers may never be determined and the figures of up to 90 per cent of the male population killed, is without support some believe. According to Stephen Pinker, "the war may have killed 400,000 people including more than 60% of the population of Paraguay, making it proportionally the most destructive war in modern times."[1] A 1999 study[2] by Thomas Whigham from the University of Georgia concluded that 150,000–160,000 Paraguayan people had survived, of whom only 28,000 were adult males. This leaves a woman/man ratio of 4 to 1, while in the most devastated areas of the nation, the ratio was as high as 20 to 1.

Of the approximately 123,000 Brazilians who fought in the Paraguayan War, the best estimates are that some 50,000 men died mostly as a result of sickness and the harsh climate. Uruguay had about 5,600 men under arms (some of whom were foreigners), of whom about 3,100 died. Argentina had almost 30,000 deaths. Uruguay had deaths of nearly 5,000 soldiers.

Memories of the war linger and in December 1975, Presidents Emesto Geisel and Alfredo Stroessner signed a treaty of friendship and co-operation in Asunción and the Brazilian government returned some of its spoils of the war to Paraguay. In April 2013, Paraguay renewed demands for the return of the "Christian" cannon that Brazil has had on display at the former military garrison, now used as the National History Museum. Brazil has refused to return the cannon, claiming it as part of its history as well.

Because López had drafted every man in Paraguay, there was no labour to work the fields, and starvation set in. Many who subsisted on bitter wild oranges succumbed to cholera, malaria and dysentery. As able-bodied men died, López recruited a new army of wounded and child soldiers. He armed them with sticks painted to look like guns, disguising the youngsters with fake beards. The army's original red uniforms had dwindled to rags; rain seeped through ponchos made of shredded carpets. Eventually they fought naked. (Today, Paraguay celebrates Children's Day on the anniversary of a battle in which 2,000 children perished.) The war's worst atrocity occurred in Piribebuy, 80km (50 miles) east of Asunción by road. There Brazilian troops cut the throats of everyone they could find, and locked the doors to a crowded hospital before setting it alight. Sexual violence during the war itself poisoned attitudes to race. In its own way, Paraguay is a melting-pot: the countryside is full of blond-haired, blue-eyed peasants who speak fluent Guaraní and halting Spanish. Yet López's propagandists tried to drum up prejudice against the Brazilian army, which was mostly black, since Pedro promised to free slaves who fought. They called the emperor the "chief of the monkey tribe". The resentment lingers. "The *kambá* raped our women," says Miguel Ángel of the Piribebuy museum, using the Guaraní word for blacks. Legend has it that the resulting black babies were killed.

Colombia

Has been constantly at war with its neighbours starting with war against Peru from 1828 to 1829 then again in 1932-33. Then war of the Supremes 1839-41. Then at war with Ecuador from 1860 to 1862.

El Salvador and Honduras war

The conflict (known as the Football War) lasted only four days, but had major long term effects for Salvadoran society. On 14 July 1969, armed conflict erupted between the two countries over immigration disputes caused by Honduran land reform laws. Trade was disrupted, causing tremendous economic damage to both nations. An estimated 300,000 Salvadorans were displaced due to battle, many of whom were exiled from Honduras; in many cases, the Salvadoran government could not meet their needs. The Football War served to strengthen the power of the military in El Salvador, leading to heightened corruption. In the years following the war, the government increased military spending and repression of the indigenous population, leading to an extended civil war, costing many lives.

The Mexican–American War

Also known as the Mexican War, the US–Mexican War or the Invasion of Mexico, was an armed conflict between the United States and the Centralist Republic of Mexico (which became the Second Federal Republic of Mexico during the war) from 1846 to 1848. It followed in the wake of the 1845 US Annexation of Texas, which Mexico considered part of its territory, despite the 1836 Texas Revolution. The war ended in a victory for the United States and the Treaty of Guadalupe Hidalgo specified the major consequence of the war: the forced Mexican Cession of the territories of Alta California and New Mexico to the United States in exchange for $15 million. In addition, the United States assumed $3.25 million of debt owed by the Mexican government to US citizens. Mexico accepted the loss of Texas and thereafter cited the Rio Grande as its national border.

The Americas have remained relatively peaceful now for a few generations and the spirit of cooperation continues throughout the region with a commitment for peaceful resolution of conflicts. An agreement to ban nuclear weapons from the region and the exclusion of North American bases in many Latin American countries hold out hope for the region.

Notes to Chapter 4

1   Steven Pinker, *The Better Angels of our Nature: A History of Violence and Humanity* Penguin, 2011, p. 238.
2   "The Paraguayan Rosetta Stone: New evidence of the demographics of the Paraguayan war, 1864-1870", *Latin American Research Review*, 1999.

Chapter 5

LEGACY OF SLAVERY AND NATIVE GENOCIDE

This chapter will attempt to fill some of the gaps left by a colonial educational system that has taught us more about European history than about the history of the vast majority of inhabitants in the Americas. It is often said that those who don't know history are doomed to repeat it. Research shows that education is an important tool in violence reduction; understanding the root causes of violent behaviour will help in finding solutions to stopping it. An awareness of the violence and its effect on some of our fore-parents will help in understanding the violent behaviour of some of our parents today. Studying our history is challenging and according to one historian, "Caribbean history is a long recitation of human suffering because the prolonged crime of African slavery that marred that history for centuries had been preceded by the genocide of the Island Arawaks."[1]

At the root of the violence in the Americas today lies this painful history. We need come to terms with it, if we are to stop the violence. This is not about guilt; that is not useful. It is so we can begin the work of repairing the damage. We have all been affected by this history of violence and recognising that it was a damaging experience is the first step in recovery. The effects are wide-ranging and still being felt: "The legacy of slavery is the dehumanisation of others and assumptions of white superiority, as well as terrible disparity of wealth and power. They could not be starker than they are today."[2]

Perpetrators of violence often minimise the violence they do and find it hard to accept that their early experience of mistreatment had anything to do with their bad behaviour. Being in denial about the hurt experienced often makes it harder for perpetrators to accept responsibility for their violence to others. Facing up to our painful past is part of the collective recovery for our communities; let us begin with a brief examination of that history.

After his euphoric "discovery" of the New World in 1492, it did not take Columbus too long to plan the subjugation of the indigenous people. After spending only his second day on the island he was busy writing to his patrons: "…unless your Highnesses should order them to be brought to Castile, or to be kept as captives on the same Island; for with fifty men they can all be subjugated and made to do what is required of them."[3]

The slave trade in the Caribbean was initiated when, on his third trip to the West Indies, Columbus shipped 600 enslaved Amerindians to Spain.[4] The replacement of outward-bound indigenous people by inward-bound Africans would see an estimated 12 to 20 million captives from Africa transported over a 300-year period to the Americas.

The destruction of the Amerindian labour force was short sighted, as one letter from King Ferdinand to Diego Columbus demonstrates "…as you know the greatest need of the islands at the moment is more Indians, so that those who go there from these kingdoms to mine gold may have Indians to mine it with. You can imagine the profit that is being lost."[5] The shortfall in labour supply would have to come from the mainland; as illustrated by the letter from Don Fray Juan de Zumarraga to Charles V, complaining about the destruction of one Mexican village by governor Nuno de Guzman, who "…had taken from it a great number of its free natives and had branded them and sold them in the islands." Not only that, he gave general license to all its inhabitants to take 20 or 30 slaves for the islands.... Nine or ten thousand souls have been removed, branded as slaves, and sent to the islands. And truly I think there were more, because about twenty-one ships sailed from there laden..." not all would arrive at their destination as "three shiploads of them have sunk and others have thrown themselves into the sea and drowned: and so would others do if they were not watched and guarded and kept in prison by the Spaniards so that they will not kill themselves."[6]

The pleas of Don Fray fell on deaf ears. Ferdinand cared little about the fate of the Indians and was more concerned about the profit he could make, writing to Diego Columbus: "...as you know all the good of those parts lies in there being a number of Indians to work in the mines and plantations"[7] and to Juan Ponce de Leon governor of Puerto Rico: "You have done me a service by your efforts to pacify the Island and by branding with the letter F on the brow the Indians captured in war, enslaving them and selling them to the highest bidder, reserving a fifth part of the proceeds for me."[8]

The Spanish conquistadors not only deployed conventional warfare, they also used deceit and trickery to enslave the Amerindians. A fleet fitted out by settlers on Hispaniola, with permission of King Ferdinand, sailed to the Lucayan islands and told the Natives there that they had come from Hispaniola "... where the souls of their parents and relatives rested and that if they wanted to see them... they would take them to it ... with these persuasive and wicked words they induced these innocent people men and women to board the ships... But on arrival in Hispaniola when they saw neither their parents nor those they loved but only tools such as spades, hoes, bars and iron sticks and the mines where they soon died and realising that they had been tricked some in despair killed themselves by drinking the sap of the bitter cassava..."[9]

That some would choose death rather than be subjected to the Repartimento-distribution of Indians to the Spaniards-is understandable. Bartolomé de las Casas complained that "Ovando dissolved the many large villages there were in this Island, and he gave to each Spaniard as many Indians as he wanted; to one 50, to another 100 and to some more and to others less, according to whether each was in his good favour; and in this number there were children and old people, pregnant women and women who had just given birth, patricians and plebeians, and the very lords and kings of their villages and country...". They would all suffer the same fate more or less the Spaniards 'took the husbands to mine gold, 10, 20, 40 and 80 leagues away and the women stayed on the plantations or farms working the soil...with sticks ...to dig holes thirty two inches deep and twelve feet wide...sweating in labour incomparably more onerous than that of miners in Castile... a hard work even for giants."[10] Families hardly saw each other for months and when they did they were too exhausted, hungry and depressed to procreate. The infant mortality rate soared in Cuba as "the mothers overworked and hungry had no milk in their breasts... some mothers drowned their children out of despair...others... took herbs to cause a miscarriage..."[11] With men dying in the mines and women on the farms and children not being born there was only one fate for the Indians, "they were all bound to die out soon, as they did, and thus, this large, valuable, fertile although unfortunate island was depopulated."[12]

Las Casas had good reason to fear for the Indians survival and fought tirelessly in their cause pleading that "...they were given little rest...he allowed cruel Spanish executions to supervise and direct them...These people treated the Indians so harshly and with such inhumanity that they seemed to be the ministers of hell, who day and night allowed not a moment of peace and rest. They beat them, slapped them, kicked them and whipped them and the Indians never heard a kinder word from them than 'dogs'."[13]

The oppression was total: "Ovando completely took away their liberty and agreed to place them under the most cruel and horrible servitude and captivity that could hardly be believed unless one saw it with one's own eyes, for the Indians were not free to do anything at all. Even the beasts are free sometimes to graze in the fields but the Spaniards did not allow the Indians to do even this...they were never free to do anything, except to go where the cruelty and avarice of the Spaniards sent them, not as captives but as beasts which their owners tied up to do with as they pleased."[14]

Las Casas, desperate to save the Amerindians from extermination, recommended the use of Africans; an action he later regretted because "...the enslavement of the Negroes was as unjust as that of the Indians and it was not a wise solution to advise the importation of Negroes".[15] Despite all his efforts, the Amerindians were wiped out in a short time from most of the Islands, forcing the Spaniards to turn to the mainland for replacements.

Initially the monarchs wanted Catholics only in the New World but the demand for labour was too great for them to hold this line for long, especially since the indigenous people were fast disappearing. The Spaniards did not turn immediately to Africa for labour; some wished to exclude "Moors, Jews and reconciled persons, their children and grandchildren ... since such persons are always evilly disposed, seditious and revolutionary in towns and communities."[16]

Prior to Columbus's discovery of the Americas, there were in the Iberian Peninsula Black or Moorish Africans who had occupied parts of Spain for generations before being defeated in 1492. Some were there either through the Arab slave trade, the Castilian and Portuguese colonization of Africa, or as free men assimilated into the population. Some of these slaves who after a time became Christianised and learnt Spanish were referred to as negros ladinos ("cultivated" or "Latinised Blacks"), as opposed to Negros bozales ("muzzled Blacks" – those captured in Africa and tied up to prevent them escaping). There were 50,000 Negros ladinos in Spain in the 15th century. The Ladinos' skills merited a higher price than for bozales. Black Ladinos born in the Americas were Negros criollos ("Creole Blacks").

The Spanish monarchs, Ferdinand 1 and Isabella, first granted permission to the colonists of the New World to import African slaves in 1501. Nicolas de Ovando wasted no time and imported the first African slaves from Spain; between 1502 and 1518 hundreds of black slaves were exiled from Castile where they had lived for generations. But the enslavement of Africans only really took off when Bartholomé de las Casas suggested it; the colonizers wasted no time in writing to the Monarch: "...would Your Highness have authority granted us to fit out vessels in this island to go to Cape Verde islands and the Guinea coast to fetch them, or have permission given to some other person from those Kingdoms to bring them hither..."[17] The monks of the Dominican Order also advocated African slavery "since the labour of one Negro was more valuable than that of four Indians".[18]

The colonisers were granted permission and in 1510 the first sizeable shipment, consisting of 250 Black Ladinos, arrived in Hispaniola from Spain. Eight years later African-born slaves arrived in the West Indies. The colony of "La Española" was organized as the Royal Audiencia of Santo Domingo in 1511. Sugar cane was introduced from the Canary Islands and the first sugar mill in the New World was established in 1516 on Hispaniola, heralding the mass influx of African slaves.

The thirst for labour, to meet the growing demands of sugar cane cultivation, accelerated the trade in Africans into a brutal system that destroyed millions of African lives in Africa, the Atlantic Ocean and in the Americas. We cannot simply brush aside this destruction of human lives with calls to "move on", as voiced by former British prime minister David Cameron in Jamaica in 2015,[19] and hope that the damage done by centuries of slavery, will simply go away. We need to examine and address the problems arising from this brutal period in our history if we are to begin to repair the damage done. Slavery has not only left negative stereotypes about Africans and Indians; it has also left its mark on white people, who often act out feelings of superiority on the indigenous and African-heritage peoples in the region today.

Some healing must take place for the oppressors and for the oppressed before we can truly move on. If our fore-parents were assessed after emancipation by today's standards, many would have been diagnosed as suffering from post-traumatic stress syndrome (PSTD). Many were in no shape to be good parents and unfortunately passed on many of the hurts they endured during slavery to their children, who in turn passed it on to the next generation. In the same way racist ideology and behaviour has been passed on among some European-heritage people, from one generation to the next.

To overcome some of the negative stereotyping of Africans and indigenous peoples, it is important that we learn about their rich culture and achievements. It is not true that Africans came to the region as slaves only, Africans made the journey as free men and women long before Columbus, as Professor Ivan Van Sertima ably demonstrated in his book *They Came before Columbus*.[20] They arrived at first by accident; as the ocean currents from West Africa directly link to the Caribbean, some of our ancestors were simply swept away in the currents, only to land in the Caribbean. There were also planned expeditions, accounting for the presence of the many relics of African art, customs and writing found in pre-Columbus Guatemala.

The African Slave Trade

The trade in Africans started as a trickle in the fifteenth century and soon became a flood lasting over 300 years, with some 12 to 20 million Africans transported from the shores of Africa, packed like sardines on slave ships off to the New World. Many had been captured, sold or tricked into slavery. Sometimes forced to walk for months, to one of the European built forts, where they were held in the most inhumane conditions imaginable, before being forced onto vessels bound for the New World. Up to one-third perished as a result of the unhealthy and brutal conditions on board, with many committing suicide by jumping into the ocean. After the transatlantic journey, which took up to three months they arrived in the Americas to learn of their new life as slaves. Thence commenced a "seasoning" process on arrival, which was to "adjust him psychologically for work as a slave and teach him the tasks and routine of plantation... would also include an attempt to break the spirit of any African, who showed signs of defiance."[21]

For the men, women and children who survived the middle passage, a lifetime of hard, brutal work was their lot, as planters speculated as to the best method to extract maximum profit from their muscle power. Many slave owners believed it was more profitable to work the enslaved to death in a short space of time, and did just that. This enforced labour demanded the use of wanton violence, to coerce the enslaved to greater efforts and to maintain control. The planters showed little mercy, resorting to medieval-type methods as they amputated, whipped, hanged, raped, burned, chained, broke at the wheel and starved the enslaved into submission.

This was capitalism at its worst – Africans treated as less than human, simply for profit. Women would be doubly exploited for sexual pleasure and sometimes for procreation. Hardly any humanity was extended to pregnant women; they worked just as hard and were subjected to the lash equally as the men. There were constant violent rebellions often ending with mass brutal punishment and horrific slaughter of slaves. This is an example of the punishment meted out to offending slaves – extracted from the session book of a single parish in Jamaica:[22]

1776: Jack, for being a runaway: "to be hanged by the neck until he is dead, and his head to be cut off in the most public place on the sd. Estate".

Coach: for "uttering many rebellious expressions" against his overseer: "to be hanged... and his head to be afterwards separated and exposed".

Adam, for running away: "to have a halter put about his neck, and one of his ears nailed to a post and that the executioner do then cause the said ear to be cut off close to his head".

Plato: for having fresh veal found upon him belonging to Roselle plantation: "to have both his ears cut off close to his head, to be worked in chains for twelve months, and ...the first Monday in every month to receive 39 lashes with a cat-o-nine tails on his bare back each time".

19 April 1783: Priscilla, for running away: "both her ears cut off close to her head immediately, to receive 39 lashes the first Monday in every month for one year and to be worked in irons during that time".

5 July 1780: Jackson for running away: "to have his right ear cut off close to his head, his nose slit, and to be branded on each cheek with the plantation mark".

1767: Quaco, for being found armed with a military offensive weapon called a cutlass and using it in a rebellious manner against one of Charlie Blair Esquire's negroes who endeavoured to catch him for being a runaway for some months: "to have both his ears cut off close to his head and also the great tendon, commonly known by the name of Tendon Achilles, of his left leg to be separated or cut asunder in such manner as it may not reunite".

The brutal experience of slavery continues to be felt, passed down through generations. One only has to reflect on the kind of violence often perpetrated by parents on children to know that some of the behaviours experienced during slavery are being acted out. Violence continues to plague all regions of the Americas, especially in the poor, black and indigenous communities. African-American women make up just 13 per cent of US American women yet comprise about half of female homicide victims, the majority of them killed by a current or former boyfriend or husband. They are victims of violence at rates 35 per cent higher than white women. Research shows that those most affected by violence are likely to come from deprived areas, have little education, face racial oppression, lack adequate housing and health care.

Resistance to slavery
The enslaved constantly fought against their miserable existence – not only individual, spontaneous acts of resistance, but often carefully planned and executed massive rebellions whenever a leader emerged. Resistance was a constant threat and the planters avoided having slaves speaking the same language working together in large gangs. Speaking in African languages was discouraged and heavy punishment was often dished out to offenders. There was resistance to slavery at every point, in Africa, on the slave ships, in the Americas, there was also resistance in Europe, by whites opposed to this reintroduction of slavery. The Quakers were often active in the resistance in Europe, but not without criticism.

Faced with opposition to the enslavement of Africans, the planters sought to justify their actions by telling blatant lies about Africans – that they were cannibals, pagan, living in trees, barely members of the human race, with smaller brains – and besides the planters were making Christians of them. These were the same tired lies told about the indigenous peoples in earlier times. At one conference in Barcelona, attended by members of the Kings Council and other clergymen, in discussing how the Amerindians should be treated, it was claimed that "these people are savages, steeped in idolatry, who sacrifice human beings, eat human flesh and deal with the devil. They practice sodomy and have many wives; their vice is drunkenness, they go about naked and know no shame and have other vices"[23] and deserved to be enslaved because:

1. The Indians are vicious, especially in their lust, gluttony and laziness; they take more pride in going off to the woods and eating roots, spiders and other filth than in the Spanish way of life. 2. If they were set at liberty, they would revert to their nakedness, idolatry and superstitions and would forget all they have been taught. They lack the capacity for living without tutelage, like Christian Spaniards; the cleverest among them is more stupid than the humblest peasant in Spain; so that liberty would be pernicious to their bodies and souls…[24]

The cumulative action of defending and justifying slavery is what developed the ideology of racism that afflicts every corner of the world today. The planters invested in spreading myth that the slaves were happy, contented and better off in the New World as slaves, than as free men in Africa. The reality was constant and numerous rebellions by the slaves throughout the Americas, for the entire period of enslavement. Every rebellion, however small, added to the ripple effect that culminated at times into bigger and bolder rebellions. These rebellions helped force the pace of emancipation as, "The evidence taken before the Committee of the two Houses of Parliament made it manifest, that if the abolition of slavery were not speedily effected by the peaceable method of legislative enactment, the slaves would assuredly take the matter into their own hands, and bring their bondage to a violent and bloody termination."[25]

Let us take a look at some of the more significant slave revolts:

Haiti.

The first major slave revolt in the Americas occurred in Santo Domingo during 1522, when slaves led an uprising in the sugar plantation of admiral Don Diego Colon, son of Christopher Columbus. Many of the enslaved managed to escape to the mountains where they formed independent communities. Increased sugar production meant more slaves and large numbers of the newly imported African slaves fled into the nearly impassable mountain ranges in the island's interior, joining the growing communities of *cimarrónes*—literally, "wild animals". By the 1530s, cimarrónes bands had become so numerous that in rural areas the Spaniards could only safely travel outside their plantations in large armed groups.

1690 Jamaica.
A formidable rebellion, involving some 500 slaves, occurred at Suttons in Clarendon. The rebels attempted unsuccessfully to hold the plantation but were forced to retreat having suffered heavy losses. Some 150 rebels, armed with guns taken from the plantation, established a strong settlement in the mountains in the centre of the island.[26]

1673 Jamaica.
A rebellion occurred on a plantation in the parish of St. Anne after which "about 200 retired to the mountains and secured themselves in difficult places...from which they were never dislodged".[27]

1728-39 Jamaica.
Worried about the number of escaped slaves and the effect their settlements were having on the rest of the inhabitants, the British decided to re-enslave or annihilate them. They sent several regiments of regular soldiers to assist the militia on the island. This action forced the maroons to come together in two main groups: "The fighting, known as the First Maroon war, continued for over a decade, at the end of which the establishment had to accept the fact that the Maroons could not be defeated. The war came to an end with two formal peace treaties. These treaties confirmed the freedom of the Maroons, provided them with lands and established an alliance."[28]

1763 Berbice (Guyana)
The Berbice slave rebellion of 1763 lasted for more than a year and is regarded as one of the most significant uprisings in the history of the Dutch Caribbean. Rivalry between the two

principal leaders, Kofi and Akara and divisions along tribal lines weakened the rebels, and contributed to collapse of the rebellion. The Europeans successfully deployed the usual tactic of divide and rule among the ranks and deployed Amerindian auxiliaries to good effect, causing the revolt to collapse "... because of a number of factors: disunity, shortage of ammunition, lack of careful planning, famine, disease, outside assistance to the colonists...but for a brief moment the Africans had assumed control over the colony...."[29]

1675 Barbados.
A conspiracy for rebellion described as "cunningly and clandestinely carried and kept in secret", involving slaves on a large number of plantations, was discovered eight days before the rebellion was to commence in the parish of St Peter, having being betrayed by a female slave. 110 were charged with conspiracy, 52 being executed of whom six were burned alive, and eleven beheaded. Five conspirators took their own lives before they could be tried.[30]

1719 St Vincent.
The "Black Caribs" (descendants of escaped Africans and aboriginal Carib Amerindians) ambushed and routed a French force of 400 men attempting to occupy the island. In 1723 they also prevented entry by a British expedition.[31]

1733 Virgin Islands.
In a rebellion on the island of St. John, 40 white people were reportedly killed.[32]

1752 Berbice (Guyana)
African-born slaves on Plantation Switzerland rebelled, but the rebellion was quelled when "creole" slaves (born in Berbice) on Plantation de Poereboom and Amerindians of the Accowai tribe were employed against the rebels.[33]

1834 St. Kitts.
Attempts by the British to extend slavery by creating "apprentices" for a further six years after declaring an end to slavery were met

with resistance throughout the region, but in St. Kitts they went on strike...'When an attempt was made to compel them to work, the strike became a rebellion. There was no loss of life, but sixteen of the leaders, including two women, were tried for rebellion. Five were deported to Bermuda, the others received from 24 to 100 lashes. The courageous resistance of these apprentices contributed materially to the decision of the British Government to recommend to the colonial legislatures the shortening of the apprenticeship period to four years. This resulted in slavery being completely abolished on 1 August 1838."[34]

Make no mistake, the brutality of chattel slavery instilled deep patterns of violent and other negative behaviour that affect our communities to this day. It is not only the African-heritage and indigenous populations that are affected by slavery; by their brutal actions, the Europeans colonists were also dehumanised by the system. This history of brutal exploitation at the very base of our societies has left us with many oppressor / oppressed patterns of behaviour that continue to blight our lives.

Legacy of slavery

One of the most damaging legacies of slavery is the perverse and endemic racism and internalised racism it has engendered all over the world. Being denied human rights and treated as property to be disposed of at will, for hundreds of years, has left many with the belief that blacks are not equal to whites. This negative perception has affected both blacks and whites, albeit in different ways, and it "would be a Herculean task to estimate the terrible ravage worked by colour psychology in Caribbean life, both past and present."[35] However, it is important to note that darker complexioned people face far more discrimination, even if experienced to a lesser extent than during the struggle for independence, when "a coloured middle group distrusted the European whites, but it feared the black mass even more".[36]

Slave society was strictly stratified and controlled by the white ruling class. The general rule was the whiter the skin, the closer to the seat of wealth and power; the darker the skin the more removed. Lighter-skinned persons occupied management positions and jobs that required dealing with the public, such as bank tellers and receptionists. There can be no doubt that each "...metropolitan culture left its special mark upon its colonial subjects, the French in Martinique, the Dutch in Suriname, the Spanish in Cuba. The English in the West Indies did likewise."[37]

Haiti

Haiti provides a good example of the kind of social stratification in existence after occupation. Founded in 1492 by the Spanish, the island eventually split into French and Spanish colonies. The French controlled Saint-Domingue in 1789 was the most profitable possession of the French Empire, producing 60 per cent of the world's coffee and 40 per cent of the world's sugar imported by France and Britain. Black slaves were the lowest class of society and outnumbered whites and free people of colour by ten to one. The slave population by 1789 was estimated at 452,000, almost half of the one million enslaved in the Caribbean at the time. Two-thirds of this population were African-born and tended to be less submissive than those born in the Americas.

Among Saint-Domingue's 40,000 white colonials in 1789, European-born Frenchmen monopolized administrative posts. The sugar planters, the *grands blancs*, were chiefly minor aristocrats. The lower-class whites, *petits blancs*, included artisans, shopkeepers, slave dealers, overseers, and day labourers. Saint-Domingue's free people of colour, the *gens de couleur*, numbered more than 28,000 by 1789. Many of them were artisans and overseers, or domestic servants in the big houses. The colonials began to fear them and sought to control them by passing discriminatory laws telling them were they could live and what clothing they could wear. They were also barred from occupying many public offices. One free man of colour who resisted this discrimination was Julien Raimond; he had been actively appealing to France for full civil equality with whites since the 1780s. He used the French Revolution to make discrimination the major colonial issue before the National Assembly of France.

Vincent Ogé, another wealthy free man of colour from the colony, returned home from Paris In October 1790, believing that a law passed by the French Constituent Assembly gave full civil rights to wealthy men of colour; he demanded the right to vote. When the colonial governor refused, Ogé led a brief insurgency in the area around Cap-Français. He was captured in early 1791, and brutally executed by being "broken on the wheel", before being beheaded. Ogé was not fighting against slavery, but his brutal killing was cited by later slave rebels as one of the factors in their decision to rise up in August 1791. The conflict up to this point on the island was between factions of whites and between whites and free blacks. Enslaved blacks watched from the sidelines.

At the same time the North American colonies, emboldened by the French revolutionaries, made a bid for liberation. Their leader, Thomas Jefferson, supported the French Revolution and the ideals it promoted; but as a Virginia slave-holder he also feared the spectre of slave revolt. Faced with the question of what the United States should do about the French colony of St. Domingue, he favoured offering limited aid to suppress the revolt but also suggested that the slave owners should aim for a compromise, similar to the one that Jamaican slave-holders made with communities of escaped slaves in 1739.

Jefferson eventually decided against support for the leader Toussaint L'Ouverture and pursued a policy to isolate Haiti, fearing that the Haitian revolution would embolden the slaves in the United States. He grew even more hostile to Haiti after L'Ouverture's successor, Jean-Jacques Dessalines, ordered the execution of whites who remained on the island; this after Napoleon with the intention of reimposing slavery attempted to reconquer St. Domingue.

Haiti, under Jean-Jacques Dessalines, declared itself independent on 1 January 1804, but had to wait until 1825 before France formally recognized Haitian independence. Jefferson refused to do so, and Haiti had to wait until 1862 for the USA to recognize them as a sovereign, independent nation.

The legacy of slavery is nowhere better exemplified than in Haiti, which has paid a high price for daring to discard the yoke of slavery. After successfully fighting off the might of the British, French and Spanish armies, the European nations and the newly independent United States of America were determined that Haiti not be seen as a success story. Haiti was subjected to the most brutal political and economic isolation, which led to stagnation and hardship for the newly freed slaves. They were eventually forced to pay 150 million gold francs in reparations to French slave holders in 1825, the price for French recognition of their independence. Although the amount of reparations was reduced in 1838, Haiti was unable to pay off its debt until 1947. The result of that extraordinary extortion, is that today Haiti is the most impoverished, uneducated, unhealthy country in the western world, despite one time regarded as the "jewel of the Caribbean". Since declaring independence, Haiti has not been allowed a moment's peace, invaded several times by the USA and currently occupied by UN troops.

But it is not only Haiti that has suffered victimisation; after emancipation, 100 years of apartheid rule prevailed in the West Indies. The Report of the West India Royal Commission, also known as The Moyne Report (enquiry into conditions in the West Indies), published in 1945, exposed the terrible living conditions for the masses living in the British West Indies. The report claimed people were denied rights, had no vote and were lowly paid, in effect the conditions people lived in were no better than those of slavery days. Little provision for education in the British West Indies meant, for example, that Jamaica started out with 82 per cent illiteracy when granted independence in 1962.

The policy to use the West Indies as a source of raw material made most of the colonies still predominantly dependent on agriculture: "One of the strongest criticisms of British Imperialism was that the colonies were regarded primarily as markets for British manufactured goods. It was a cause of complaint that local industries which would produce goods to replace or compete with imports from Britain were prohibited or discouraged."[38]

The Apartheid-like system in the British Caribbean placed whites firmly in political and economic control. The clamour for independence forced them to make concessions to the mainly light-skinned population; who inherited most of the economic and social power at the granting of independence. However, their "pro-British alignment, combined with their anxiety to deny their African heritage, made them into social and political enemy of the black masses, a few liberal individuals excepted. They were the carriers of, perhaps more than any other group, of the "white bias" of the society".[39]

The most damaging legacy of slavery is perhaps the development of an ideology of racism that persists to this day – an ideology that has limited the life chances of African and Indigenous peoples of the Americas in a profound way, as evidenced by the fact that they still make up the vast majority of the disadvantaged people in the region and the world – more likely to live in poor housing, more likely to have poor education, more likely to suffer from mental ill health, more likely to die young, often from curable disease. More likely to be addicted to mind-altering drugs. More likely to be imprisoned, more likely to be blamed for the condition they find themselves in. The material existence that racism has forced upon blacks and indigenous people is not the only damage done; it could be argued that an even more damaging legacy is the effects of "internalised racism" afflicting the lives of many black and indigenous people.

The historian Richard Hart summed it up thus:

The system of enslavement rested just as much, or even more so, upon a collection of related ideas, values, attitudes and behaviour that were forcibly and consistently articulated by the dominant institutions of society including the church, administration, judiciary, police, legislature, newspapers, and plantation. The latter was so dominant that scholars almost unanimously described it as a total Institution. These official institutions demeaned, defamed and outlawed African culture, ethnically cleansed history of African achievement and so assassinated African identity and ultimately disabled Africans in ways that still retard development. On the other hand Europe was incorrectly proffered as the source of everything good; in a word, inherently superior. The majority of oppressors and oppressed alike were inculcated with these lies and so a society was created where race mattered more than anything else in the determination of most people's fortunes.[40]

There was a deliberate attempt to destroy and distort African history by claiming that Africa had no civilisation or written word. On the contrary, in many instances African civilisation was far more advanced than that of the West, as argued by Walter Rodney:

> Under the patronage of the Fatimid Dynasty (969 AD to 1170 AD), science flourished and industry reached a new level in Egypt. Windmills and water wheels were introduced from Persia in the 10th century. New industries were introduced- paper making, sugar refining, porcelain and the distillation of gasoline. The older industries of textiles, leather and metal were improved upon. The succeeding dynasties of the Ayyubids and the Mamuluks also achieved a great deal, especially in the building of canals, dams, bridges and aqueducts, and in stimulating commerce with Europe. Egypt at the time was still able to teach Europe many things and was flexible enough to receive new techniques in return....The Fatimids founded the city of Cairo, which became one of the most famous and most cultured in the world, seat to the legendary 'Arabian Knights'. At the same time they established the Azhar University which exists today as one of the oldest in the world.[41]

Derogatory myths about Africa and Africans were spread by the planter class supported by journalists, philosophers, religious leaders, writers, psychologists, etc. Their reach was far and wide and has permeated much of the world with racist ideology. It is only by challenging these myths that we can restore a sense of pride in things African. Some outstanding scholars from the region and beyond have not only exposed the lies created and spread by those who set out to exploit African labour, but have illuminated the great achievement of African civilisations. One only has to look at the many outstanding artefacts, culture, scientific inventions and achievements in all spheres of life to know that Africans have no superiors.

Racism

Often discourse on racism is problematic because usually there are no clear understanding and/or agreement, of terminology used. For the purpose of clarity "racism" when used here, is meant the systematic one-way mistreatment of a group of people based on the colour of skin. Racism implies power. Only people with power can exercise racism; for example, they can deny jobs, housing, education or freedom of movement. In white dominated society whites have this power to be racist to black people. When this power is exercised by the state it is deemed to be "institutional racism". Black people can also be racist in black dominated communities, where they hold power. Then there is racialism; one can be racialist – that is, being prejudiced towards someone with a different skin colour or culture – but this does not imply power, although it may cause hurtful things to be said or done. When white people react to black people as threatening or regard them as shifty, criminals and lazy – common stereotypes for black people – they are being racist. Scientists in the 1950s declared that race as a concept makes little sense, as the differences between people are so small, as to be of little or no significance.

The real significance of highlighting racial differences is for the economic exploitation of a people. This was the motivation behind the ideology of racism developed in European countries ready to exploit the labour and resources of the African and indigenous peoples of the Americas. This ideology developed and propagated over centuries has infected the whole world. Research has shown that white people living in remote areas, with no contact with black people whatsoever, have negative racist beliefs, which they could only have learnt from the media. These same negative attitudes towards black people have often been "internalised" by many black people:

Internalised racism

When Black people believe the negative things said about them and behave or think on the basis of those negatives; this is what constitutes internalised oppression. The negative stereotyping of black people, internalised by so many, is responsible for much of the low self-esteem, and bad feelings that many black people harbour. The effect of the constant stereotyping of black people as being violent, causes many to act out this stereotype and this is the source of much of the black on black violence. When black people internalize the harmful and negative stereotyping of blacks and act it out on each other, that is internalized racism at work. It often manifests in extreme criticism of other black people. It has been shown that black children choose white dolls over black ones because they see them as better than black ones – a result of the negative imaging of black people on television.

Black people had little chance to heal from the effects of white racism they experienced during slavery and colonialism. Much of the bad effects of this racism has been passed on down generations. Most people working in the parenting field agree that parents usually raise children the way they were themselves parented. If they were beaten as children they tend to hit their children and often defend their actions as "it did me no harm". Although parenting skills are improving there are instances where extreme brutality is still being passed on to children – one of the root causes of much of the violence in our society today.

Institutional racism is when the state colludes with racism and uses its power to negatively affect the lives of black people. For instance black people are six times more likely to be stopped and searched than whites by the police in Britain.[42] The gunning down of blacks in the USA by the police is another instance of extreme institutional racism. The state also has an impact on black people's education, health, housing and employment.

In all of the countries in the Americas, racism, internalized racism and institutional racism is in full operation. Economic exploitation is at the root of most oppression; treat people as less than and pay them less. Social and employment discrimination against indigenous and black people is widespread with the International Labour Organization reporting that employers in the region paid indigenous workers 32 per cent less than non-indigenous workers. Employers also frequently did not afford indigenous workers basic rights provided by the labour laws such as a minimum wage.

Nowhere is the legacy of slavery more felt than in Brazil where the Ministry of Labour fined 340 Brazilian companies from May 2013 to May 2015 for using slave labour, including forced labour, and people working in degrading conditions, for little or no pay in rural and urban areas. Brazil, the largest importer of enslaved Africans, abolished slavery in 1888 – some 50 years after slaves were freed in the Caribbean – but "there are still pockets of Brazil, especially on farms and in areas where the Amazon jungle is being razed, where working conditions are similar to those in the 19th century, experts say."[43] Brazil officially recognised the active use of slave labour in 1995 when the Labour Ministry launched a Special Mobile Enforcement Group that works with prosecutors and police to find and raid farms, construction sites and other companies suspected of employing slave workers. Government figures reveal that around 50,000 people have been freed since operations began.

Deep-seated discrimination has meant the impoverishment of black and indigenous populations. A 2011 household survey of eight Latin American countries found seven per cent of the population that is neither indigenous nor Afro-descendant is indigent or highly vulnerable to indigence, a percentage that rises to 11 per cent in the case of Afro-descendants and to 18 per cent among indigenous peoples. Similarly the Economic Commission for Latin America and the Caribbean (ECLAC) said while 62 per cent of the non-indigenous and non-Afro-descendant population was considered to be not vulnerable; this figure rises to 56 per cent in the case of Afro-descendants and to just 33 per cent among indigenous people. In the same vein in the region, women accounted for 51 per cent of the population but only access 38 per cent of the total income that people generate and earn, with the remaining 62 per cent going to men. 18 per cent of all employed people earn incomes that are below the poverty line in Latin America and the Caribbean according to ECLAC data from 17 Latin American countries from 2013.[44]

There can be no doubt that slavery and native genocide has had a devastating negative impact on the Americas. The poverty, lack of education, poor housing and health care prevalent in indigenous and black communities has undoubtedly hampered development. There is a need to repair the damage done by conquest, enslavement and colonization if the region is to develop its full potential. The notion that Native Americans and Africans are lesser than whites runs deep and needs to be addressed, if we are to bring about true equality. Understanding how racism and internalized racism stunts the personal, political and economic development of our communities, will help build better communities.

Slavery as a system, existed in ancient times in most countries of the world, but the reintroduction of chattel slavery with white owners and black victims was very different from what had passed before, as the Africans "...were separated from their masters not only by servitude but by a chasm of different customs, culture, religion and physical appearance. Their liberated descendants, still identifiable by their colour, and nursing resentful memories of bondage, stand on the edge of that chasm to this day; and many bridges have still to be built to span its frightening depths."[45]

The work of repairing the damage done by slavery has hardly begun. The affluent nations need to be reminded that the world's wealth was built on the blood, sweat and tears of the indigenous people and enslaved Africans. From the days when the indigenous people were forced to strip the gold and silver mines, making Spain one of the richest countries in the world, the Americas provided the labour and natural resources for much of the wealth generated globally. Eric Williams in *Capitalism and Slavery* argues that the enslavement of Africans in the West Indies to produce sugar on the plantations stimulated the Industrial Revolution in Britain:

> The slave trade kept the wheels of metropolitan industry turning; it stimulated navigation and shipbuilding and employed seamen; it raised fishing villages into flourishing cities; it gave sustenance to new industries based on the processing of colonial raw materials; it yielded large profits which were ploughed back into metropolitan industry; and, finally it gave rise to unprecedented commerce in the West Indies and made the Caribbean territories among the most valuable colonies the world has ever seen.[46]

Sir Hilary Beckles demonstrated in his book *Britain's Black Debt* how "The Lascelles, a lower middle class family from the hinterland of Leeds, began modestly with a small slave-owning operation in Barbados in 1648, but within one hundred years, had accumulated one of the largest fortunes in the British Empire. With this financial base they gained access to the English aristocracy. The Earls of Harewood, as they became known, did not dispose of their sugar plantation in Barbados until 1975,"[47].

In spite of the wealth created for the Europeans, little consideration was paid to the educational, social or economic development of the masses of black people during or after emancipation. It is instructional that the Spanish colonists established Universities not long after colonisation of the New World, while not a single university was built in the English colonies. The contempt with which the slaves were held was reflected in the fact that the British compensated the white slave owners for the loss of their property and paid not one penny for the newly emancipated slaves.

And to add insult to injury, when the British government realised the full cost of paying £20 million in compensation to the slave owners, they tried to recoup some of their losses by extending slavery by another six years. In this time they reckoned the "apprentices" would have earned enough to cover the full cost of compensation. Now they do not even consider their brutal extraction of wealth from Africans for over three hundred years, as deserving of an apology – regrets, of course! but reparations for slavery? Too long ago! They can't remember! But the records stand and we now know who received how much and for whom, thanks to the sterling work of Catherine Hall and her associates at the University of Westminster. As the voices for reparations for slavery grow stronger by the day, it will be interesting to see how long the British government can resist the demands for justice.

Defeating racism

Throughout much of the Americas, and especially in the USA, power is held by white people. They have been able to use this power to impose their will on the rest of the Americas for most of the last century and a half. The tide is turning slowly: the imperialist project is beginning to run out of steam as more and more Latin American countries resist the white power they see emanating from the USA. All US citizens benefit from this imperialism but it is a tiny minority – the one-percenters, as they have been dubbed – who benefit mostly, becoming richer day by day. Neo-liberal policies wreak untold suffering on the vast majority of the peoples and the environment of the Americas. Understanding how racism affects black people's lives is something that white Americans will have to inform themselves about. It is their responsibility and ultimately in their interest to put an end to racism. The solution is not to bury heads in the sand, as did the recently elected "I say nothing" President Donald Trump when he was questioned about racial healing in the US presidential debate with Hillary Clinton on 22 September 2016. Working together as black and white we can end racism and herald a new beginning for the Americas. Let's get to work!

Notes to Chapter 5

1   Walker, *Columbus and the Golden World of the Island Arawaks*, p. 34.
2   Catherine Hall, "The racist ideas of slave owners are still with us today", *The Guardian*, 22 September 2016.
3   Williams, *Documents of West Indian History*, p. 52.
4   Williams, *From Columbus to Castro*, p. 31.
5   Williams, *Documents of West Indian History*, No. 69, p. 69.
6   Williams, *Documents of West Indian History*, p. 68.
7   Williams, *Documents of West Indian History*, No. 70, p. 69.
8   Williams, *Documents of West Indian History*, No. 71, p. 69.
9   Williams, *Documents of West Indian History*, p. 66.
10 Williams, *Documents of West Indian History*, No. 95, p. 100.
11 Williams, *Documents of West Indian History*, No. 95, p. 100.
12 Williams, *Documents of West Indian History*, No. 95, p. 100.
13 Williams, *Documents of West Indian History*, No. 95, p. 100.
14 Williams, *Documents of West Indian History*, No. 95, p. 101.
15 Williams, *Documents of West Indian History*, No. 152, p. 157.
16 Williams, *Documents of West Indian History*, No. 39, p. 37.
17 Williams, *Documents of West Indian History*, No. 126, p. 142.
18 Williams, *Documents of West Indian History*, No. 127, p. 142.
19 Rowena Mason, "Jamaica accuses David Cameron of misrepresenting prison transfer deal", *The Guardian*, 13 October 2015.
20 Van Sertima, *They Came Before Columbus*, 1976.
21 Richard Hart, *Slaves Who Abolished Slavery Volume 1, Blacks in Bondage*, University of the West Indies, 1980, pp. 86-87.
22 Richard Hart, *Occupation and Control – The British in Jamaica – 1660-1962*, Kingston, Jamaica: Arawak Publications, 2013, pp. 69-70.
23 Williams, *Documents of West Indian History*, No. 118, p. 133.
24 Williams, *Documents of West Indian History*, No. 119, p. 134.
25 Richard Hart, *The Abolition of Slavery*, Community Education Trust, 1989, reprinted by Caribbean Labour Solidarity, 2007, in conjunction with Karia Press, 2007, p. 39, quoting from Henry Bleby, *Death Struggles of Slavery* (3rd edition), London, 1868, p. 117.
26 Hart, *Abolition of Slavery*, p. 50.
27 Hart, *Abolition of Slavery*, p. 49.
28 Hart, *Abolition of Slavery*, p. 53.
29 W. F. McGowan, James G. Rose and David A. Granger (eds), *Themes in African-Guyanese History*, Hansib, 2009, p. 103. Alvin O. Thompson, *The Berbice Revolt 1763-64*.
30 Hart, *Abolition of Slavery*, p. 49
31 Hart, *Abolition of Slavery*, p. 52.
32 Hart, *Abolition of Slavery*, p. 53.
33 Hart, *Abolition of Slavery*, p. 54.
34 Hart, *Abolition of Slavery*, p. 64.
35 G. K. Lewis, *The Growth of the Modern West Indies*, London: MacGibbon & Kee, 1968, p. 67.

36 Lewis, *The Growth of the Modern West Indies*, p. 87.
37 Lewis, *The Growth of the Modern West Indies*, p. 69.
38 Richard Hart, *Towards Decolonisation*, Canoe Press, University of the West Indies, 1999, p. 107.
39 Lewis, *The Growth of the Modern West Indies*, p. 77.
40 Richard Hart, *Caribbean Workers Struggles*, Bogle-L'Ouverture Publications, Socialist History Society, 2012, introduction, p. 3.
41 Walter Rodney, *How Europe Underdeveloped Africa*, Bogle-L'Ouverture Publications/Tanzania Publishing House, 1972, pp. 58-59.
42 Hayden Smith, "Black people six times more likely to be stopped and searched by police", *The Independent*, 27 October 2016.
43 Thompson Reuters Foundation, Bogotá, February 2016.
44 *The Antigua Daily Observer*, 8 November 2015.
45 Henry Marsh, *Slavery and Race: The Story of Slavery and its Legacy for Today*, Canada: Douglas David & Charles Limited, 1974, p. 78.
46 Williams, *From Columbus to Castro*, 1970, p. 148.
47 Hilary M. C. D. Beckles, *Britain's Black Debt*, University of the West Indies Press, 2013, p. 122.

Chapter 6

CIVIL WAR AND ITS LEGACY OF VIOLENCE

Civil war has ravaged much of Latin America for much of the late 20th century and has had a profound effect on the levels of violence prevalent in the region today. The highest crime and murder rates recorded in the region are in the countries that experienced some of the worst excesses of extremely violent acts, often perpetrated by dictatorial regimes upon their own citizens. The loss of life is one concrete measure of the suffering these wars have inflicted, but the effects of the repression on society as a whole is harder to measure. Of the communities most affected by the violence, it is likely that many suffer from what is now recognised as post-traumatic stress disorder (PTSD). With no treatment for this serious mental health condition, the likely outcome is yet more senseless violence; as it is believed that people who have been exposed to violent trauma and receive no treatment are more likely to act out violence on themselves or on others close to them.

War is a nasty brutal business, especially for the men on the front line of battle, with many combatants left to deal with the trauma of battle on their own and as research has shown, prone to use violence after they have left the theatre of war. A recent study in Britain has shown that one in eight returning veterans have attacked someone after returning home, with those who witnessed two or more traumatic incidents more likely to be violent than those who did not.[1]

The problems arising from the use of violence do not stop at the victims; perpetrators of the violence are also affected, as Guillermo Reyes Rammsy, a former conscript to the Chilean army, demonstrated. He called a talk-show host to confess his role in the murder of 18 opponents of Chilean dictator Augusto Pinochet, revealing that he was feeling suicidal. He confessed to having executed political prisoners: "I participated in 18 executions...We shot them in the head and then blew up the bodies with dynamite, there was nothing left, not even their shadow." he told the talk host.[2]

Defeating domestic violence will require zero tolerance to all forms of violence, including state-sanctioned violence. As long as societies continue to depend on men fighting, domestic violence will remain a problem. Socialization for violence is what makes men behave in violent ways; sexist conditioning from society as a whole is what makes it likely that men will act out violence on women. The research could not be clearer: violence breeds violence, and it has also been shown that the rate of domestic violence goes up in countries that are engaged in war.[3]

In our relatively short history, the Americas has been almost continually at war. We have had pre-historic tribal war followed by native genocide, slavery, the wars for independence, inter-regional wars, Banana wars, civil wars and now the drug wars; all have left deep scars on the psyche of the region. We have to come to terms with this history of violence if we are to learn lessons, heal our communities and move towards non-violent societies. "For more than two decades, Latin Americans have been looking to locate their dead and find their missing children. Latin Americans have also gradually concluded that they must prosecute the perpetrators of evil, if they are to achieve peace and closure in their societies. 'Nunca Mas' has become a rallying cry in the region."[4]

The recent civil wars in the region have seen some of the worst acts of violence committed against innocent civilians. It comes as no surprise that the "Northern Triangle" Central American countries of El Salvador, Guatemala and Honduras, which were subjected to some of the worst "cold war" atrocities, are at the top of the list of violent countries today. War is damaging for civilians but it also deeply affects veterans as studies have shown that many are unable to continue in relationships or make new ones.[5] Veterans also make up a large proportion of the homeless, imprisoned, those locked up in mental health institutions, and drug addicts. We will now briefly turn our attention to civil wars in the region to raise awareness of the extent of the violence experienced.

Argentina

The Dirty War 1976-83 (part of Operation Condor) was the name used by the Argentinian government for the seven years of state terrorism in Argentina against political opponents. Military and security forces targeted left-wing guerrillas, political dissidents, and anyone believed to be associated with socialism.

Declassified documents of the Chilean secret police cite an official estimate of 22,000 killed or "disappeared" between 1975 and mid-1978 by the Batallon de Inteligencia 601. The National Commission on the Disappearance of Persons estimates that around 13,000 were disappeared. "Argentines were left aghast when, on 9 March 1995, Captain Adolfo Scilingo, confessed on a popular television news show that he had participated in two of the weekly 'flights', dumping thirty living but drugged desaparecidos into the South Atlantic."[6]

Victims of the violence include an estimated 15,000 to 30,000 left-wing activists and militants, among them trade unionists, students, journalists, Marxists, Peronist guerrillas and alleged sympathizers. There are disturbing stories of torture and inhumanity unspeakable, including "parents had delivered to them by security forces the body of their daughter with a rat sewn inside her vagina".[7] How a family begins to recover from such a traumatic experience is hard to imagine; we can only work to ensure that such brutality never occurs again in our region.

Colombia

The Colombian conflict began about 1964, between the Colombian government, paramilitary groups and crime syndicates on one side and left-wing guerrillas, notably the Revolutionary Armed Forces of Colombia (FARC), and the National Liberation Army (ELN) on the other. The problem historically rooted in the conflict known as La Violencia, was triggered by the 1948 assassination of political leader Jorge Eliecer Gaitan. The struggle by the indigenous people for land and justice in the 1960s, was viewed as being communist inspired by the United States government, as a result they supported the anti-communist onslaught in rural Colombia. The sustained attack on civilians forced liberal and communists militants to come together to resist under one umbrella.

The justification for the fighting varied from group to group. The FARC and other guerrilla movements claimed to be fighting for the rights of the poor in Colombia, to protect them from government violence and to provide social justice through communism. The Colombian government claimed to be fighting for order and stability, and seeking to protect the rights and interests of its citizens. The paramilitary groups claimed to be reacting to perceived threats by guerrilla movements. Both guerrilla and paramilitary groups have been accused of engaging in drug trafficking and terrorism. All of the parties engaged in the conflict have been criticized for numerous human rights violations.

According to a study by Colombia's National Centre for Historical Memory, 220,000 people died in the conflict between 1958 and 2013, most of them civilians. (177,307 civilians and 40,787 fighters) and more than five million civilians were displaced and forced to migrate to other territories between 1985 and 2012.

This, one of the longest civil wars in the region in recent times, and seemed to be concluded with the signing by President Juan Manuel Santos and Rodrigo Londono, a top commander of FARC, to end the 52-year war on 21 September 2016, only to be thwarted by a referendum that rejected the deal. The war, which claimed the lives of more than 220,000 people and caused widespread destruction, with some eight million displaced, had to wait a short while longer as it was finally sanctioned by Congress on 1 December 2016. President Santos was awarded the Noble Peace Prize for signing the peace deal.

Chile
Chile's long history of civil wars goes back to the days of Bernardo O'Higgins, who ruled from 1817 to 1823 as supreme director or president. He won recognition for defeating the royalists, but his attempts at consolidating power for himself eventually led

to civil war. O'Higgins liberal land reform policies angered the Catholic Church and the owing class who seized the opportunity to mount a coup against him, when he used government funds to aid the liberation of Peru. Higgins was eventually forced to flee to Peru, where he died in 1842.

There were constant change of governments in Chile during the 1820s and during the presidency of the Liberal, Ramón Freire Serrano, slavery was abolished in 1823 – long before other countries in the Americas.

The Chilean Civil War of 1891

Also known as the Revolution of 1891 was armed conflict between forces supporting president Jose Manuel Balmaceda and forces supporting Congress. The Navy- supported Congress defeated the President, who was supported by the Army. Balmaceda committed suicide on 18 September 1891, the day his term as president expired. Loss of life during the conflict estimated at 5,000.

The 1973 Chilean coup d'état

Was against the elected socialist President Salvador Allende by the right-wing Congress, which was supported by US President Richard Nixon.[8] Allende was overthrown by the armed forces and the national police, who formed a junta that suspended all political activity and repressed all left-wing movements. Allende's appointed army chief, Augusto Pinochet rose to power within a year of the coup, seizing power in 1974. The coup is viewed as one of the most violent events in Chile's history.

In the first months after the coup the military killed thousands of Chilean Leftists and imprisoned 40,000 political opponents in the National Stadium. The coup leaders arrested more than 130,000 people in a three-year period, and the dead and disappeared numbered thousands in the first months of military government. Among those killed was Alberto Bachelet, the father of President Michelle Bachelet. It was not only political leaders and activists who were targeted; thousands of innocent citizens were tortured, killed, or disappeared during the repression.

Costa Rica

The conflict in Costa Rica started when the Legislature attempted to keep the government opposition from office by voting to annul the result of presidential elections. They claimed the opposition candidate Otilio Ulate had won the election fraudulently.

Army commander, Jose Figueres disagreed and rebelled against the government. The Civil war lasted for 44 days from 12 March to 24 April 1948 with an estimated 2,000 killed. The government was defeated and Figueres ruled Costa Rica for a year and a half as head of a provisional government junta. He abolished the military, which was unpopular because it had been used in clashes with civilians previously; and oversaw the election of a Constitutional Assembly. Ulate won the elections, the junta stepped aside and Costa Rica has been one of the most peaceful countries in the region since. Costa Rica was also instrumental in bringing peace to Central America, when President Oscar Arias succeed in convincing the other four Central American leaders to sign the Esquipulas II Peace Accord on 7 August 1987, bringing an end to the civil wars.

Dominican Republic

Civil war erupted in the Dominican Republic in 1903, 1904, and 1914; the country was later occupied by the United States of America from 1916 to 1924. The US occupation began on 13 May 1916 when Rear Admiral William B. Caperton forced the Dominican Republic's Secretary of War Desiderio Arias, who had seized power from Juan Isidro Jimenes Pereyra, to leave Santo Domingo by threatening the city with naval bombardment. Three days after Arias left, United States Marines landed, took control of the country within two months and imposed a military government. A guerrilla movement, known as the "gavilleros", fought against the US occupation from 1917 to 1921. Their defeat paved the way for the dictatorship of Rafael Trujillo, which stretched from 1930 until his assassination in May 1961.

In December 1962 the Dominican Republic held its first free elections in almost four decades. The victor, Juan Bosch, promised social reform, but the Kennedy administration decided that he was soft on Communism and brought about his downfall with the help of the military in September 1963. Some young officers rebelled against the coup and on 24 April 1965 announced that they would return Bosch to the presidency; the population came out in their support. Urged on by Washington, "loyalist" generals attacked the capital, the stronghold of the revolt, only to be defeated by thousands of armed civilians and hundreds of rebel soldiers. The US alleged that Communists had gained control of the revolt and President Lyndon B. Johnson sent in the troops. A four-month stalemate ensued with the rebels holding out in downtown Santo Domingo. The United States and the Dominican government it had created controlled the rest of the country. Eventually in September 1965 a provisional government was established and elections followed in June 1966.

Casualties: 13 US soldiers killed, 200+ wounded. Versus 500 guerrillas killed 100 captured, 3,000 civilians killed.

El Salvador

Civil War in El Salvador (1979–92) was a conflict between the military-led government of El Salvador and the Farabundo Marti National Liberation Front (FMLN).

The conflict has its roots in the late 19th century, at a time when coffee was a major cash crop for El Salvador, bringing in approximately 95 per cent of the country's income, which benefited only two per cent of the population, leaving the vast majority living in poverty. Socio-economic tension grew throughout the 1920s, and was compounded by a drop in coffee prices following the 1929 stock-market crash. In 1932, the Central American Socialist Party was formed and it led an uprising of peasants and indigenous people against the government. The government brutally suppressed the uprising in what became known as the 1932 Salvadoran peasant massacre or simply "La Matanza" (the Massacre), with the military murdering between 10,000 and 40,000 Indians. Farabundo Marti, the leader of the uprising, was eventually arrested and killed in 1932, as the military subsequently took control of the country.

This was one of the most brutal civil wars in the region. This is how the Catholic paper *Socorro Juridico* reported on a 50-day period at the end of June 1980, when more than 2,500 Salvadorians were tortured, assassinated or massacred:

"The cruelty of tortures practiced against the victims of the repression had no precedent in the previous. The corpses appeared scalped, beheaded, with throats cut and dismembered. The heads of the decapitated began to appear hung from trees or impaled on fences. In addition to the paramilitary -based repression, large scale military operations were mounted in the north and central-east regions of the country. Massacres included that of women and children fleeing from the country to seek refuge in Honduras. In September "there were reports of indiscriminate bombing attacks on villages and the use of heavy artillery and helicopter gunships. Some 5000 troops were deployed in an operation against a guerrilla stronghold in Moragan; an estimated 3,000 civilians were reported to have died in that operation.... the death toll for 1980 reached at least 13,000 by December."[9]

This kind of violent trauma would have affected huge swathes of the population and with little chance of healing, it is not surprising that some of the worst kinds and levels of violence are perpetrated in El Salvador today.

During the conflict, in February 1980 Archbishop Oscar Romero published an open letter to President Jimmy Carter, pleading with him to suspend the US support for the military. A month later, on 24 March 1980, the Archbishop was assassinated while celebrating mass, the day after he had called upon Salvadoran soldiers and security force members to not follow their orders to kill civilians. At his funeral a week later, government-sponsored snipers shot 42 mourners. On 7 May 1980, former Army Major Roberto D'Aubuisson was arrested with a group of civilians and soldiers at a farm. The raiders found documents connecting him and some civilians as organizers and financiers of the death squad who killed Romero.

The atrocities continued, with the rape and murder of four American nuns and a laywoman on 2 December 1980. Members of the Salvadoran National Guard were suspected to have killed the Maryknoll Missionary nuns Maura Clarke and Ita Ford, the Ursuline nun Dorothy Kazel, and laywoman Jean Donovan.

They were on a Catholic relief mission providing food, shelter, transport, medical care, and burial to death squad victims. The United States reacted by cutting off military aid to pacify the critics, but within six weeks the aid was renewed.

As government-sanctioned violence increased, resistance grew and in May 1980, the Salvadoran revolutionary leadership met in Havana and formed a consolidated politico-military command, which became the Farabundo Martí National Liberation Front (FMLN) in honour of insurgent hero Farabundo Marti. The FMLN immediately announced plans for an insurrection against the government and mounted their first major attack on 10 January 1981.

The response of the outgoing President Carter administration was to increase military aid to the Salvadoran armed forces to $10 million, which included $5 million in rifles, ammunition, grenades and helicopters. In justifying the arms shipments, the administration claimed that the regime had taken "positive steps" to investigate the murder of the four American nuns; but their own Ambassador, Robert E. White disagreed, saying that "there never was and there never has been a serious investigation of the deaths."[10]

It is estimated that the army and security forces killed 16,000 civilians over the course of 1981. That year, Amnesty International identified "regular security and military units as responsible for widespread torture, mutilation and killings of non-combatant civilians from all sectors of Salvadoran society." The report also stated that the killing of civilians by state security forces became increasingly systematic, with the implementation of more methodical killing strategies, which allegedly included use of a meat packing plant to dispose of human remains. Between 20 August and 25 August 1981, there were 83 decapitations reported. The murders were later revealed to have been carried out by a death squad using a guillotine.

In late 1981, the Atlacatl Battalion, created in 1980 at the US Army School of the Americas in Panama, was deployed in a major stronghold of the FMLN. On 11 December 1981, they occupied the village of El Mozote and massacred at least 733 and possibly up to 1,000 unarmed civilians, in what became known as the El Mozote

Massacre. The Atlacatl soldiers accused the adults of collaborating with the guerrillas. The field commander said they were under orders to kill everyone, including the children, who he asserted would grow up to become guerrillas if they let them live. "We were going to make an example of these people," he said.

The slaughter continued and on 10 June 1982, almost 4,000 Salvadoran troops carried out a "clean-up" operation in the rebel-controlled Chalatenango province. More than 600 civilians were reportedly massacred during the Army sweep. The Salvadoran field commander acknowledged that an unknown number of civilian rebel sympathizers or "masas" were killed, in what he declared a success. 19 days later, the Army massacred 27 unarmed civilians during house raids in a San Salvador neighbourhood. The women were raped and murdered. Everyone was dragged from their homes and executed in the street.

Death squads

Despite mostly killing peasants, the government readily killed any opponent they suspected of sympathy with the guerrillas – clergy (men and women), church lay workers, political activists, journalists, labour unionists, medical workers, liberal students and teachers, and human-rights monitors. The State's terrorism was executed by the security forces, and the paramilitary death squads gave the government cover for their political killings. Typically, a death squad dressed in civilian clothes and travelled in anonymous vehicles with dark windows and blank license plates. They terrorised people by publishing future-victim death lists, delivering coffins to said future victims, and sending the target person an invitation to his/her own funeral.

Truth Commission

At the end of the war, the "Commission on the Truth for El Salvador" held between January 1980 and July 1991, registered more than 22,000 complaints of political violence; 60 per cent of the complaints were about summary killing, 25 per cent about kidnapping, and 20 per cent about torture. These complaints attributed almost 85 per cent of the violence to the Salvadoran Army and security forces alone. The Salvadorian Armed Forces were accused in 60 per cent of the complaints, the security forces (i.e. the National Guard, Treasury Police and the National Police) in 25 per cent, military escorts and civil defence units in 20 per cent of complaints, the death squads in approximately 10 per cent, and the FMLN in 5 per cent. The report concluded that more than 70,000 people were killed. More than 25 per cent of the populace was displaced as refugees before the U.N. brokered peace treaty. On 16 January 1992, the Chapultepec Peace Accords were signed in Chapultepec Castle, Mexico City, ending the war in El Salvador.

Guatemala

Although indigenous Guatemalans constitute more than half of the national populace, they have been dispossessed of their lands since colonial times by the descendants of Spanish and other European immigrants and by some of those with mestizo ancestry. In the late 19th and early 20th centuries, Guatemala's fertile land was exploited by foreign companies, chief among them the United Fruit Company, which enjoyed the support of the US government and Guatemalan authoritarian rulers and wealthy landowners, who facilitated the exploitation of the indigenous landless by brutal labour regulations.

In 1944, General Jorge Ubico's 13-year dictatorship was overthrown by the October Revolutionaries, a group of Guatemalan nationalists made up of military officers, university students and liberal professionals. Widespread civil unrest, sparked by a soldier killing a school teacher, precipitated the coup d'état deposing General Ubico, who surrendered power to a military junta of his generals. Further civil unrest prompted two officers, Captain Jacobo Arbenz Guzman and Major Francisco Javier Arana, to lead a final coup, deposing the dictatorship of the generals.

The victorious army officers quickly stepped aside as promised and allowed general elections, heralding The Ten Years of Spring, a democratic period of free speech and open political activity. Juan José Arévalo was elected President in 1945 and served until 1951. A former university professor, Arévalo introduced social reforms, such as allowing the free establishment of political parties, and the restricted establishment of trade unions.

Agrarian reform, which sought to redistribute the land for agricultural purposes, was implemented by the government in 1953. This angered the United Fruit Company (UFC), which continued to hold thousands of acres in pasture, as well as substantial forest reserves. The Guatemalan government had offered the company compensation for the appropriated land, but the company fought the land expropriation, demanding twenty times more than the Guatemalan government had offered. The UFC opposed the progressive social and economic reform programme of the government and lobbied the US government for their overthrow. Declassified CIA documents show that the US government organized, funded, and equipped the 1954 coup d'état, deposing the elected Guatemalan presidential government of Jacobo Arbenz Guzman.

Ongoing social discontent in the 1960s gave rise to a series of armed leftist movements, emerging from the large populations of indigenous people and peasants. The Guatemalan security forces responded with forced disappearances, the number of "disappeared" reaching into the tens of thousands by the end of the war. In 1970, the first of many military rulers representing the Institutional Democratic Party, took office and repression increased. During the 1980s, the Guatemalan military assumed almost absolute government power for five years.

The Civil War ran from 1960 to 1996, mostly fought between the US-supported government of Guatemala and various leftist rebel groups, supported mainly by ethnic Mayan indigenous people and Ladino peasants. It was mainly a large-scale campaign of one-sided violence by the government against the civilian population of indigenous activists, suspected government opponents, returning refugees, critical academics and students, left-leaning politicians, trade unionists, journalists, and street children.

Between the years of 1966 and 1968 alone, some 8,000 peasants were murdered by the US-trained forces of Colonel Arana Osorio. Sociologist Jeffrey M. Paige alleges that Arana Osorio "earned the nickname 'The Butcher of Zacapa' for killing 15,000 peasants to eliminate 300 suspected rebels".

Up to 200,000 people died or went missing during the war, including 40,000 to 50,000 who "disappeared". Felipe

Cusanero became the first person convicted by the Guatemalan courts in 2009 and sentenced for the crime of ordering forced disappearances.

Following the end of the war in 1996, Guatemala re-established a representative democracy but it has since struggled to enforce the rule of law and suffers a high crime rate, as well as continued extra judicial killings, often executed by security forces. In 2013, the former dictator Efrain Rios Montt was put on trial for genocide, for the killing and disappearances of more than 1,400 indigenous Ixil Mayans during his 1982-83 rule. The first former head of state to be tried for genocide by his own country's judicial system, Montt was found guilty and sentenced to 80 years in prison but within two weeks his cronies in the constitutional court overturned the conviction on a technicality.

During Ríos Montt's tenure, civilians are reported to have been beheaded, garrotted, burned alive, bludgeoned to death, or hacked to death with machetes. More than 250,000 children nationwide were estimated to have lost at least one parent to the violence; in El Quiche province alone these children numbered 24,000. In many cases, the Guatemalan military specifically targeted children and the elderly. Soldiers were reported to have killed children in front of their parents by smashing their heads against trees and rocks. Amnesty International documented that the rate of rape of civilian women by the military increased during this period, including rape of pregnant women.

It is hard to comprehend the effect of witnessing violent acts such as, "Four Indian campesinos were taken prisoner in El Quiche. Soldiers drove stakes into their rectums, their ears, their mouths, their eyes. Then in front of their horrified families and the rest of the village, they were burned alive." Or in Quiche, where 60 men were rounded up in San Juan Cotzal and killed in front of their families and friends. Or of 12 peasant women assassinated and decapitated in Uspantan.[11]

A renewed peace process (1994-96) saw elections in November 1995. Alvaro Arzu Irigoyen was elected and under his administration peace negotiations were concluded. The government and the guerrilla umbrella organization URNG (Unidad Revolucionaria Nacional Guatemalteca), which became a legal party, signed peace accords ending the 36-year internal conflict in December 1996. The General Secretary of the URNG, Comandante Rolando Moran, and President Alvaro Arzu jointly received the UNESCO Peace Prize for their efforts to end the civil war and attaining the peace agreement.

The UN-sponsored Historical Clarification Commission (CEH) in a 1999 report blamed the state for 93 per cent of the human rights violations committed during the war, the guerrillas for 3 per cent. The victims of the war were 83 per cent Maya. "The Terror in Guatemala is far from being a thing of the past; instead it exists in the memories and daily lives of millions of survivors, and it continues to manifest in systemic racism, discrimination and violence against the Indigenous majority."[12]

Honduras

Officially the Republic of Honduras is located in Central America and was at times referred to as Spanish Honduras (differentiating it from British Honduras, which became the modern-day state of Belize). It became independent of Spanish rule in 1821 and has been a republic since breaking away from the Central American Federation in October 1938. As an independent state it has had no fewer than 300 small internal rebellions and civil wars in the country.

The United Fruit Company and Standard Fruit Company dominated the country's key banana export sector. To protect American interests in this "Banana republic" (a term coined by writer O. Henry in 1904 to describe Honduras) US troops invaded in 1903, 1907, 1911, 1912, 1919, 1924 and 1925. The country became a key base for US President Reagan's war on Revolutionary Nicaragua.

A military coup, with the backing of the Supreme Court in 2009, removed the reformist-minded president Manuel Zelaya, who it was feared was being influenced by the late President Chavez of Venezuela. His illegal removal to Costa Rica plunged the country into instability, poverty and gang- and drug-related crime. This led to a sharp increase in murders, from an already high of 61 per 100,000 in 2008, to 90 homicides for every 100,000 in 2012, earning Honduras the dubious record of having the most murders per capita in the world. The election of Juan Orlando Hernandez in 2013 has seen the violence plunge to figures of 57 homicides in every 100,000 in 2015.

Mexico

The Mexican Civil War, or the Mexican Revolution, was a major armed struggle that started in 1910, with an uprising of land owners, rural campesinos, the church, the bandit Pancho Villa and campesinos leader Emiliano Zapata against the 35-year-long dictatorship of Porfirio Diaz. The conflict lasted for the best part of a decade, with the loss of 2 million lives from a population at the time of 15 million.

After the overthrow of Diaz in 1911 Madero was elected president. He failed to implement promised land reform and was assassinated in 1913. The following two years saw liberal leaders Venustiano Garranza and Alvaro Obregon assume power and implement some of the demands of the revolutionaries, including land reform under a new 1917 Constitution. Oil and mineral deposits were nationalised and the State and Church were separated under the new constitution.

The revolution lost steam with the assassination of Zapata in 1919 and the laying down of arms of Pancho Villa, who made peace with the new government of Obregon. The new government brought some stability before Obregon was also assassinated in 1928. Obregon's assassination led to the creation of the Partido Nacional Revolucionario (National Revolutionary Party) in 1929, which galvanized all opposition groups, excluding the Conservatives and Catholics. It was renamed the Partido Revolucionario Institucional (Institutional Revolutionary Party) (PRI) in 1946 and they monopolized power through the 20th century, until the general elections of 2000.

The Dirty War refers to the internal conflict between the Mexican PRI-ruled government and left-wing student and guerrilla groups in the 1960s and 1970s. The conflict began as a result of attacks on the 1968 student rally in Mexico City, in which 30 to 300 were killed, according to official reports; non-governmental sources claim thousands were killed. During the war, government forces carried out disappearances estimated at 1,200.

Nicaragua

After intermittent landings and naval bombardments in the previous decades, Nicaragua was occupied by the United States of America almost continuously from 1912 to 1933, when the conservative government of Adolfo Diaz asked the USA for support during an insurrection. In 1914, the Bryan-Chamorro Treaty was signed, giving the USA control over a proposed canal, as well as leases of land for potential canal defences.

In 1926 the Marines returned to Nicaragua after a nine-month absence, when violent conflict erupted between the Conservative and Liberal forces. From 1927 until 1933, General Augusto Cesar Sandino led a sustained guerrilla war, first against the Conservatives then against the US Marines. Before the marines withdrew in 1933 they helped set up the National Guard, a combined military and police force, trained and equipped by the Americans.

After the retreat of the Marines, Sandino was tricked by the Sacasa government, who invited him to the presidential house under the pretext of dinner and signing a peace treaty. The National Guard captured and killed him when he left the presidential house on 21 February 1934. Hundreds of his followers were later captured and executed by the National Guard.

Nicaraguan Revolution (1960s-1990)

Carlos Fonseca founded the Sandinista National Liberation Front in 1961 in the name of the fallen historical figure Sandino, and eventually took power in July 1979. The deposed dictator Somoza fled the country but was eventually assassinated in Paraguay in September 1980. In response to the Sandinistas coming to power, a number of opposing groups came together as the "contras". They had the support of U.S President Reagan, whose administration authorized the CIA to help the rebels with funding, armament and training. The contras operated out of Honduras and Costa Rica.

The contras engaged in a campaign of terror against the rural Nicaraguan population, using murder, rape and torture on a huge scale. They were supported by a USA campaign of economic sabotage, which included mining the harbour to disrupt shipping. A full trade embargo was also in place, while they accused the Sandinistas of human rights abuses.

Despite the hostilities, Daniel Ortega won the 1984 presidential election, which was judged to be free and fair, but criticised as a "sham" by the Reagan administration. With wilful disregard of a ruling by the US Congress, the murderous contra continued to receive full backing of the Reagan administration. The International Court of Justice in regard to the case of Nicaragua v. United States of America in 1984 found: "The United States of America was under an obligation to make reparation to the Republic of Nicaragua for all injury caused to Nicaragua by certain breaches of obligations under customary international law and treaty-law committed by the United States of America". During the war between the Contra and the Sandinistas, 30,000 people were killed. Thirty years have passed and Nicaragua is still awaiting an apology and reparations from the USA.

Peru

Peru won independence from Spain in 1824, but was ruled by an aristocratic oligarchy of Spanish descent well into the early 20th century. Intermittent periods of democratic development were interrupted by autocratic military rule before mass party politics developed, in the latter half of the 20th century. Resistance to military rule led to insurrection by the Revolutionary Left Movement (MIR), which was defeated by 1965 but another guerrilla movement called *Sendero Luminoso*: the Shining Path, rose to prominence in the 1980s.

Founded in the late 1960s by Maoist-inspired philosophy professor Abimael Guzmán, the Shining Path grew from a small radical cell to a guerrilla army numbering over 10,000 combatants. It used insurgency tactics and terrorist attacks against military and civilians targets, in an attempt to defeat the Peruvian government. Guzmán was an isolationist who refused to align his movement with foreign powers and even refused to work with the second-most prominent leftist group in Peru, the Tupac Amaru Revolutionary Movement (MRTA).

The civil war saw multiple parties compete for control over overlapping territories and constituencies. No part of the country was untouched by the conflict, but the worst violence was concentrated in the Andean highlands, where guerrilla and government forces terrorized the native population. Shining Path fighters allegedly hacked their victims to death with machetes in order to save ammunition. Government and paramilitary forces unleashed waves of torture and sexual violence and even massacred entire villages. One such massacre near the village of Accomarca killed 69 civilians, including children and the elderly.

In July 2001, a Truth and Reconciliation Commission (CVR) was convened to investigate the human rights abuses that took place between 1980 and 2000. The CVR's final report, published in August 2003, found that the war had caused an estimated 69,000 deaths and disappearances, the majority of whom were indigenous civilians. The number of dead and disappeared was more than the casualties of all other wars in modern Peruvian history.

Uruguay

The Uruguayan Civil War, or the Guerra Grande ("Big War"), was a series of armed conflicts that took place between the liberal Colorado Party and the National Party in Uruguay from 1839 to 1851. The two parties received backing from foreign sources including both neighbouring countries such as the Empire of Brazil and the Argentine Confederation as well as imperial powers, primarily the British Empire and the Kingdom of France, a legion of Italian volunteers including Giuseppe Garibaldi was also involved.

In the early 1960s, an urban guerrilla movement known as the Tupamaros formed, at first robbing banks and distributing food and money in poor neighbourhoods, then undertaking political kidnappings and attacks on security. In 1965 the US Office of the Public Safety (OPS) began operating in Uruguay, and trained Uruguayan police and intelligence in policing and interrogation techniques. They were also reported to have trained the police to torture victims using electrical implements. [13]

President Jorge Pacheco declared a state of emergency in 1968, and this was followed by a further suspension of civil liberties in 1972 by his successor, President Juan Maria Bordaberry who used the Army to combat the guerrillas of the

Movement of National Liberation (MLN). After defeating the Tupamaros, the military seized power in 1973. Torture was frequently used against trade union officers, members of the Communist Party and even regular citizens, in order to gather information on the MLN. Uruguay soon had the highest per capita percentage of political prisoners in the world and torture continued to be used, until the end of Uruguayan dictatorship in 1985.

Around 180 Uruguayans are known to have been killed during the 12-year military rule from 1973 to 1985. Most were killed in Argentina and other neighbouring countries, with only 36 of them having been killed in Uruguay. A large number of those killed, were never found and joined the list of the "disappeared".

United States of America

The Civil War is a defining event in America's history. The Revolution of 1776-83 may have given birth to the United States, but it has been argued, the Civil War of 1861-65 determined the kind of nation it would be. The war helped to resolved two fundamental questions thrown up by the revolution: whether the United States was to be a dissolvable confederation of sovereign states or an indivisible nation with a sovereign national government; and whether its declaration, that all men were created with an equal right to liberty, could be sustained while it was the largest slave-holding country in the world.

The Civil War started because of unresolved differences between the free and slave states over the power of the national government to prohibit slavery in the territories that had not yet become states. Abraham Lincoln won the 1860 election on a platform pledging to keep slavery out of the territories, as a result seven slave states in the Deep South seceded and formed a new nation, the Confederate States of America. Lincoln and most of the Northern people refused to recognize the legitimacy of secession and war eventually broke out.

Northern victory in the war preserved the United States as one nation and ended the institution of slavery that had divided the country from its beginning. But these achievements came at the cost of 625,000 lives – the largest and most destructive conflict in the Western world between the end of the Napoleonic Wars in 1815 and the beginning of World War I in 1914.

Venezuela

The Federal War (1859–63) – also known as the Great War or the Five Year War – was a civil war between the conservative party and the liberal party over the monopoly the conservatives held over land and government positions, and their reluctance to grant any reforms. This drove the liberals to look for greater autonomy for the provinces and it led to the biggest and bloodiest civil war Venezuela had since its independence. In a country with a population of just over a million people at the time, hundreds of thousands died in the violence of the war, or from hunger or disease. Hostilities ended with the signing of the Treaty of Coche in April 1863.

The Venezuela Crisis of 1902–03 was a naval blockade from December 1902 to February 1903 imposed against Venezuela by Britain, Germany and Italy over President Cipriano Castro's refusal to pay foreign debts and damages suffered by European citizens in the recent Venezuelan civil war. Castro assumed that the United States' Monroe Doctrine would see the USA prevent European military intervention, but at the time the USA interpreted the Doctrine as concerning only European seizure of territory. With prior promises that no such seizure would occur, the USA allowed the European action to go ahead without objection. The blockade saw Venezuela's small navy quickly disabled, but Castro refused to give in, and instead agreed in principle to submit some of the claims to international arbitration, a condition he had previously rejected. Germany initially objected to this, particularly as it felt some claims should be accepted by Venezuela without arbitration.

US President Theodore Roosevelt forced the Germans to back down by sending his own larger fleet and threatening war if the Germans landed. With Castro failing to back down, US pressure and increasingly negative British and American press reaction to the affair, the blockading nations agreed to a compromise, but maintained the blockade during negotiations over the details. This led to the signing of an agreement on 13 February 1903 that saw the blockade lifted, and Venezuela commit 30 per cent of its customs duties to settling claims.

The Permanent Court of Arbitration in The Hague awarded preferential treatment to the blockading powers against the claims of other nations, the USA feared this would encourage future European intervention. To counter this risk they came up with the Roosevelt Corollary to the Monroe Doctrine, asserting the right of the United States to intervene to "stabilize" the economic affairs of small states in the Caribbean and Central America, if they were unable to pay their international debts.

Banana wars

These were a series of occupations, police actions, and interventions involving the US in Central America and the Caribbean between the Spanish-American War (1898) and the inception of the "Good Neighbour Policy" (1934). These military interventions were often carried out by the United States Marine Corps, who were involved so often they developed a manual in 1921, *The Strategy and Tactics of Small Wars*. On occasion, the Navy provided gunfire support and Army troops were also used.

By the Treaty of Paris, Spain handed over control of Cuba, Puerto Rico, and the Philippines to the United States. Thereafter, the USA conducted military interventions in Panama, Honduras, Nicaragua, Mexico, Haiti and the Dominican Republic. The series of conflicts only ended when President Franklin D. Roosevelt ordered the withdrawal of troops from Haiti in 1934. The conflicts were largely economic in nature. They were called "Banana wars" because they were connected with the preservation of US commercial interests in the region. The most prominent, the United Fruit Company, had significant financial stakes in production of bananas, sugar cane, tobacco and various other products.

One of the most active military officer in the Banana Wars was US Marine Corps, Major General Smedley Butler, who saw action in Honduras in 1903, served in Nicaragua enforcing American policy from 1909 to 1912, was awarded the Medal of Honor for his role in Veracruz in 1914, and a second Medal of Honor for bravery while "crush(ing) the Caco resistance" in Haiti in 1915. In 1935, Butler wrote in his famous book *War is a Racket*:

> I spent 33 years and four months in active military service and during that period I spent most of my time as a high class muscle man for Big Business, for Wall Street and the bankers. In short, I was a racketeer, a gangster for capitalism. I helped make Mexico and especially Tampico safe for American oil interests in 1914. I helped make Haiti and Cuba a decent place for the National City Bank boys to collect revenues in. I helped in the raping of half a dozen Central American republics for the benefit of Wall Street. I helped purify Nicaragua for the International Banking House of Brown brothers in 1902-1912. I brought light to the Dominican Republic for the American Sugar interests in 1916. I helped make Honduras right for the American fruit companies in 1903. In China in 1927 I helped see to it that Standard Oil went on its way unmolested. Looking back on it, I might have given Al Capone a few hints. The best he could do was to operate his racket in three districts. I operated on three continents.

Hot on the heels of the banana wars was the "Cold War" between the Soviet Union and the United States of America often fought out in the "backyard" of the USA;

During the cold war, the United States destabilised governments in Argentina, Bolivia, Brazil, British Guiana, Chile, the Dominican Republic, Ecuador, El Salvador, Guatemala, Nicaragua and Uruguay. It tried but failed to destabilise two other countries, Cuba and Haiti, and worked to strengthen repressive military-dominated regimes, like the Honduras of the 1980s, and police states, like Uruguay of the 1970s.[14] It also invaded the little island of Grenada.

With the recent signing of the peace treaty in Colombia ending all wars in the Americas there is a real opportunity for the region to come together as a beacon of peace in the world. If Europe can come together after two world wars; there is no reason we in the Americas cannot live in peaceful co-existence for the benefit of all its citizens. Costa Rica has set the gold standard by abolishing its army; let's all aim for gold.

There is a history of intervention in the region that our leaders must learn from if they are to avoid the pit falls. Divide and rule has long been the strategy for creating and maintaining systems of oppression and inequality. We have come a long way, and the problems before us are small compared with those we have seen off in the region. Let us be bold in taking the next steps to make our region the most peaceful in the world. Let us invoke the memory of the Island Arawak every time we are presented with challenges for peaceful co-existence.

Notes to Chapter 6

1 Hayden Smith, "One in eight war veterans is violent on return home", *Metro*, 15 July 2012.

2 Jonathan Franklin in Santiago, "Former Chilean soldier charged with murder after stunning radio confession", *The Guardian*, 11 December 2015.

3 Aronson, *The Social Animal*, 1992: researchers Dane Archer and Rosemary Gartner compared the crime rates of countries at war for roughly 110 countries since 1900; p. 258.

4 Professor Stephen G. Rabe, *Cold War Memories: Latin America versus The United States*, University of Texas at Dallas, p. 4.

5 US Department of Veteran Affairs website. A. Matsakis, *Back From The Front: Combat Trauma, Love and the Family*, Sidan Press, 2007.

6 Rabe, *Cold War Memories*, p. 7.

7 Rabe, *Cold War Memories*, p. 2.

8 Peter Kornbluh, *Chile and the United States: Declassified Documents Relating to the Military Coup, September 11, 1973*.

9 Jenny Pearce, *Under the Eagle*, Latin American Bureau, 1981, p. 236.

10 Pearce, *Under the Eagle*, p. 241.

11 Pearce, *Under the Eagle*, p. 196.

12 Paley, *Drug War Capitalism*, AK Press, 2014, p. 173.

13 Uruguayan Chief of Police Intelligence Alejandro Otero told a Brazilian paper in 1970.

14 Rabe, *Cold War Memories*, p. 3.

Chapter 7

EXTENT OF DOMESTIC
VIOLENCE IN THE AMERICAS

A recent report by United Nations Women found that many Latin American countries experience higher-than-average incidence of domestic violence. According to the agency, a woman is assaulted every 15 seconds in São Paulo, Brazil's largest city. In Colombia, attacks in which acid is thrown at women's faces nearly quadrupled between 2011 and 2012. Of the 25 countries in the world that are "high" or "very high" in the UN's ranking for "femicide" (killings of women that seem related to their gender), more than half are in the Americas, with El Salvador rated the worst in the world.

There is ample evidence that the problem of violence to women is widespread, with all socio-economic classes affected. With research showing the less educated more likely to commit acts of violence, we should not be surprised to find higher levels of violence in countries with high rates of illiteracy. As part of any strategy to defeat domestic violence it is imperative that governments invest in education as one of the measures in combating violence to women.

The intention in this chapter is to highlight the extent of domestic violence in the region so we have a better picture of the scale of the problem faced. Some of the figures quoted may not be the most recent, as these are likely to fluctuate. For those seeking the most up to date facts and figures, I recommend visiting government websites for information on the subject.

The focus here is mostly on the violence done to women, but it would be remiss to ignore violence done to men, and especially that the figures of men reporting domestic violence in the region are on the increase. Women's socialization for violence has been steadily increasing, with more and more movies depicting women as violent. This, and the rise in popularity of women boxing in the region, is helping to create a stereotype of Latino women as violent.

The region has recently experienced several large demonstrations protesting the problem of violence against women. As I write, women are protesting the killing of a young woman in Argentina. Brazil has recently faced similar protest. Let us now look at the scale of domestic violence facing some of the countries of the Americas.

Anguilla

This British Overseas Territory with a population of 14,000 passed its domestic violence Act in 2014. Few cases of domestic violence are ever reported to the authorities, although a survey by UNICEF found that 46 per cent of those surveyed believed that domestic violence "was a major problem": 34 per cent knew someone who was abused and 24 per cent knew someone who was abused and did not report it. It is believed that few reports are made because of stigma, fear of more violence and financial dependency on the abuser.

Antigua and Barbuda

A press release on 12 September 2012 by the Antigua and Barbuda government notes that violence against women in Antigua is of a "systemic nature" and that "our people are socialised to normalize and accept these patterns". There have been no studies conducted into the prevalence of women experiencing domestic violence. However, the *Antigua Observer* reported that the Gender Affairs Directorate recorded 219 cases of domestic violence and sexual violence in 2014 and 206 cases between January and October 2015.

Argentina

Like most countries in the world, Argentina has a serious domestic violence problem, with women's groups citing machismo and patriarchy as being responsible for the violence. In Buenos Aries Province, the special Women's Police Stations and Family's police stations received a daily average of 53 complaints of domestic violence.

Argentina does not have a national registry of statistics on domestic violence, but information compiled from the media shows 295 deaths in 2013 and 277 in 2014 resulting from domestic violence. An online survey was reported to have revealed that 95% of women had been in a "violent situation that deserved attention from authorities".[1] A report published in 2015 by the Domestic Violence Bureau (OVD) of Argentina's Supreme Court of Justice recorded a steady increase in domestic violence: 9,920 cases in 2013, followed by 10,252 cases in 2014 and 11,273 domestic violence-related complaints in 2015. The main perpetrators were ex-partners, recorded at 46 per cent, followed by common-law spouses at 18 per cent and spouses committing 14 per cent of the violence.

Bahamas

The murder rate in the Bahamas has more than doubled in the past decade and in 2014 was one of the highest rates in the Caribbean, at 31.9 per 100,000. The victims are mainly males aged between 18 and 25 years of age. There are no surveys on domestic violence in the Bahamas but the Royal Bahamas Police Force said that domestic violence was responsible for 14 per cent of the homicides. Non-fatal domestic violence was responsible for on average 28 per cent of all assaults reported to the police between 2011 and 2013.[2]

No specific figures for domestic violence could be found, but the 2014 crime report by the police showed an overall decrease in crime reported. Of 618 arrested for the second quarter of 2014, 512 were male and 106 female. Those aged 18-25 were the most frequently arrested. Crimes against the person fell by 8.5 per cent except for sexual assault, which rose by 4 per cent.

Barbados

It is generally accepted that figures for Domestic violence in Barbados are exceedingly limited. The creation of a Family Conflict Intervention Unit (FCIU) established by the police in 2013 has produced some figures. According to the Inter-American Development Bank (IDB) report there were 220 cases of domestic violence reported to the FCIU between June and

December 2013, and 423 cases reported in 2014. In November 2016 the *Daily Nation* newspaper reported that police logged 435 reports of domestic violence cases between January and 31 October 2016.

Belize

In 2010 there were a total of 1,477 cases of domestic violence reported in Belize, 16 per cent of victims were males. A survey conducted by the Women's Circle of Belize in 2010, found that 23 per cent of women questioned had been abused by their partners. Some 6 per cent of the respondents were hospitalized as a result of the abuse. The survey also showed that 54.3 per cent knew a victim of domestic violence.[3]

Bermuda

No official studies on domestic violence could be found, but according to the Bermuda Health Disparities Report of 2013, one in eight adults in Bermuda has experienced domestic abuse. The executive director of Bermuda's Centre Against Abuse revealed in 2014 that domestic abuse was a "big problem that goes unreported". She added: "In January we get maybe 50 calls for the month but in June and July it can be up in the 90s."[4]

Bolivia

According to the Center for the Information and Development of Women (CIDEM), 70 per cent of women suffer some form of abuse. CIDEM noted that the statistics "did not reflect the full magnitude of the problem of violence against women" and that "a great number of women" did not report the aggression they faced on a daily basis. The most exhaustive national survey on domestic violence conducted by the National Statistical Institute in 2003 showed 64 per cent of women suffered some form of emotional, physical or sexual abuse from their partner. A recent Al-Jazeera report claimed Bolivia has the highest rate of domestic violence in Latin America at a staggering 90 per cent.[5] The Bolivian attorney general's office reported that 94 women were killed in 2016 and 93 women were killed in 2015.[6]

Brazil

The government-sponsored study Map of Violence of 2012 and its additional notes on female homicides in Brazil, found that between 1980 and 2010, there were 91,930 women murdered in Brazil; 43,486 of these homicides occurred solely in the past decade. From 1996 to 2010, the average number of murders of women remained stable at around 4.5 homicides for every 100,000 women.

In relation to statistics on murders of women, Brazil ranked seventh in a ranking of 84 countries, they came behind El Salvador, Guatemala, Russia and Colombia. Within Brazil, the states with the highest rates of violence against women are Espírito Santo, Alagoas and Paraná, respectively, with rates of 9.4 (more than double the national average), 8.3 and 6.3 homicides for every 100,000 women. Among the capital cities, the highest rates are in the Northern Region: Porto Velho, Manaus and Rio Branco. Of all the female murders, 40 per cent of these incidents occurred inside the family home or residence. By comparison, the portion of male murders occurring inside the family residence stood at 14.7 per cent.

Brazilian government agency the Data Senado, responsible for the collection and interpretation of national data, conducts a yearly survey on family and domestic violence against women. Its February 2011 survey, based on 1352 interviews with women in 119 municipalities, including all the capitals and the Federal District, showed that knowledge about the Maria da Penha Law was growing: 98 per cent said they had heard of the law, against 83 per cent in 2009. Not all women report abusers, with fear remaining the main reason (68 per cent). The fact that the victim can no longer withdraw the complaint at the police station also acts as a reason for failing to report the offender, according to 64 per cent of women interviewed. Some 57 per cent of respondents reported knowing women who have suffered some type of domestic violence.

The type of violence that stands out most is physical violence, cited by 78 per cent; moral violence comes in second, with 28 per cent, almost tying with psychological violence, cited by 27 per cent. In 66 per cent of cases, those responsible for the attacks were husbands or partners. The majority of battered women, 67 per cent, reported that they no longer live with the abuser. Nevertheless a significant proportion, 32 per cent, still does, and, among these, 18 per cent of the women concerned continue to suffer attacks. Among those who said they still live with the aggressor and still are victims of domestic violence, 40 per cent reported being assaulted rarely, but 20 per cent said they suffer attacks on a daily basis.

According to Data Senado-2013, one in five women who have been assaulted have done nothing about it. The research suggests that fear and shame are factors in the non-reporting of the offence. Also recent research by the Federal University of Rio de Janeiro and the Ministry of Justice pointed out that 80 per cent of women who are victims of violence do not want their aggressors to be detained. Instead of prison, victims prefer that their perpetrators were subjected to medical care, psychological treatment or penalty payment.[7]

Cayman Islands

According to crime statistics released by the Royal Cayman Police Services, the number of serious crimes such as murder, robberies, attempted murder, rape, attempted rape, and assaults stayed about the same from year to year. Overall crime figures for 2016 increased by about 15 per cent, largely due to a reported increase in more minor crimes, including theft, damage to property, threatening violence and common assault. Reports of domestic violence went up "a whopping 82 percent" when compared with 2015.[8]

Chile

Violence against women is prevalent across all classes of Chilean society and in the early 1990s, it was reported that domestic violence affected about 50 per cent of Chilean women. Consistent with these findings, a 2003 Chilean national survey indicated that 25-30 per cent of female homicides occur at home. Women are the most likely to become victims of domestic violence, but other members of the household are also at risk. A 2004 Chilean National Women's Service (SERNAM) study reported that 50 per cent of married women had suffered spousal abuse, 34 per cent reported having suffered physical abuse, and 16 per cent reported psychological abuse. Between January and November 2005, 76,000 cases of family violence were reported to the police: 67,913 were reported by women, 6,404 by men, and approximately 1,000 by children.

Colombia
The Institute for Legal Medicine and Forensic Science reported approximately 33,000 cases of domestic violence against women during 2006 but noted that only a small percentage of cases were brought to its attention. Every hour an average of nine new acts of sexual violence against women and girls in Colombia are recorded. Thirty-seven per cent of Colombian women, according to a 2010 state-sponsored survey, report suffering violence at the hands of their intimate partners. For displaced women and girls, available evidence strongly suggests that the prevalence of these and other forms of gender-based violence is even higher: up to almost one in two displaced women, according to one survey conducted by USAID and Profamilia.

Costa Rica
A national survey on violence to women by the University of Costa Rica in May 2004 found that 58 per cent of the 908 women interviewed said they had suffered at least one incident of sexual or physical violence in the previous 16 years.

An increase in domestic violence was recorded at the public hospitals of the Social Security System, or Caja. According to the report, domestic violence increased by one-third from 2013, with 9,823 cases rising to 13,036 cases in 2015. This represented a 33 per cent increase over three years. The highest numbers seen at Caja hospitals were for physical violence, of which 52 per cent were women. The male victims were aged under 19. The highest rates of domestic violence were recorded in rural areas.[9]

Cuba
No figures for domestic violence could be found in Cuba but the secretary of the National board of the Cuban Jurists Association was quoted "I'd say its not as large as some people think or as small as we would want".

Cuban sociologist and academic Clotilde Proveyer believes that 70% of the women murdered in Cuba had prior relationship with the killer, she explained that "not appearing as separate figures, many gender crimes are lumped into general crime categories" The result she believes "is that they are made invisible."[10]

Dominica
Statistics from the Central Registry of Domestic Violence show that between July 2011 and October 2015 over 1,041 cases of domestic violence were recorded in Dominica. Of the total, 88 per cent involved violence against women, with 52 per cent of the women being younger than 16 years of age.

Dominican Republic
International Day for the Elimination of Violence against Women is observed as a result of the killing of three sisters in the Dominican Republic. Three of four sisters were killed on 25 November 1960, by General Rafael Trujillo of the Dominican Republic (DR). The victims nicknamed Las Mariposas (The Butterflies) were Patria Mercedes Mirabal, Argentina Minerva Mirabal and Antonia Maria Teresa Mirabal. The sisters were conspiring with their husbands to violently overthrow Trujillo. They have received many honours posthumously, and have many memorials in various cities in the Dominican Republic. Their home province Salcedo, changed its name to Provincia Hermanas Mirabal (Mirabal Sisters Province).

Despite their celebration, 55 years on, gender-based violence is the fourth highest cause of death among women in the DR. The UN Committee on the Elimination of Violence against Women denounced the high incidence of sexual and domestic violence against women in the DR and urged the country to develop a national action plan to fight it.

More than a thousand women have been killed in the last five years. In the majority of cases the perpetrators were intimate partners of the victims. Some 62,000 complaints of gender violence against women were reported in the Dominican Republic in 2010, according to the Prosecutor for Woman

Affairs Roxanna Reyes [11] "We cannot go much further, we're living it day to day, with cases which we didn't see five years back." Just four per cent of charges against perpetrators went on to legal trials.

Ecuador

The Office of Gender in the Ministry of Government, reported 68,184 cases of sexual, psychological, or physical mistreatment of women during 2006. In 2013 alone, 300 cases of femicide were registered nationally. The president of the National Assembly, Gabriela Rivadeneira, at a press conference to promote a campaign to Prevent Violence against women in 2016 announced that 6 of every 10 women have suffered from psychological or physical abuse and a quarter of women have been raped. A survey revealed that "38 percent of women have been physically abused, 26 percent sexually abused and 17 percent have been victims of patrimonial violence, which involves the destruction of material goods."[12]

El Salvador

According to a UN report, domestic violence in El Salvador is a "serious" and "widespread" problem, and a "large portion of the population considered domestic violence socially acceptable".[13] Between 2003 and 2014, homicide rates for women increased from 7.4 to 19.1 per 100,000 women, one of the highest rates in the world. In a 2008 national survey on family health, 31 per cent of women interviewed declared they have been subjected to physical violence before the age of 18. The same study revealed that 44 per cent of women who had been married or lived with a partner had suffered psychological violence, 24 per cent physical violence and 12 per cent sexual violence.[14]

Some of those with responsibility for protecting citizens are often guilty of abuse of power; six women were killed by their partners, who were police officers in 2012.[15] In the first months of 2013, six police officers were accused of violence against their partners.[16]

Women have been granted equal rights under the constitution, but are often subjected to discrimination in employment and other areas. Abortion is punishable by imprisonment, even when the life of the mother is at risk. The Criminal Code affirmed this law in 2013, stating that the "rights of the mother cannot be privileged over the foetus." As a result many women have been imprisoned for pregnancy-related crimes.

The Women's Association for Dignity and Life, also known as Las Dignas (Worthy Women), a Salvadoran feminist organization, noted that women do not report domestic violence as a result of "family and community pressure not to reveal domestic problems; …fear of retaliatory violence by partners; poor awareness of rights among victims; lack of sufficient support services; and low confidence in the justice system" [17]

French Guiana

French Guiana has been declared France's "deadliest department" where violence has been steadily increasing since the 2000s, especially in the capital – Cayenne. According to the United Nations in 2009 the annual murder rate of French Guiana 13.3 per 100,000 inhabitants compared with 1.1 per 100,000 in mainland France. Like most Caribbean countries reliable figures for domestic violence are hard to come by, but the levels of societal violence would indicate that domestic violence is as prevalent here as anywhere else in the region.

Grenada

According to women's rights monitors, domestic violence remains a serious and persistent problem in Grenada. The Central Statistical Office reported 462 cases of domestic violence, with 388 of the cases against women and 74 against men. However, domestic violence remains under-reported as women feared retribution, stigma or further violence.

Guadeloupe

Guadeloupe has France's highest crime rate at 8.2 per 100,000 it is slightly higher than that of Paris but much lower than most islands in the Caribbean. A report commissioned by the interior ministry and its overseas counterpart describes the "impregnation of Guadeloupian society by violence" and the "development of violent gangs". The legacy of slavery was blamed for some of the violence.[18]

Guatemala

Guatemala has the region's highest rate of femicide; at 6 per 100,000 it ranks with South Africa and Russia. Of the 80 deaths of women recorded in 2013, 66 per cent of the women were killed by firearms, 13 per cent were burned or bled to death, and 11 per cent were asphyxiated; there was also an increase in the number of decapitations. It was reported that there were nine more deaths than the previous January, with an increase in the number of young girls killed. The figures also highlight an increasing number of young girls being killed, some of them were under the age of 11 and some killed alongside their mothers.

Guyana

Despite lack of reliable figures for domestic violence in Guyana, it is recognised as a serious problem within the country and is ranked among countries having the highest incidents of abuse in the world. A recent spate of murder/suicide cases has only served to confirm this perception.

The Guyana Police Force stated that it had investigated 2,811 reports of domestic violence at the end of 2008; of these only 579 charges were made and presented to the courts, with 299 cases referred to the Probation and Social Security services.

Kaiteur News reported that at least 74 people, including 16 women, were murdered between January and 11 June 2015. Statistics released by the police show a 12 per cent rise in homicides and a 10 per cent rise in serious crimes in the first five months of 2015. The Force's Public Relations Department stated that 66 murders were recorded at the end of May 2015, by comparison with 59 murders at the end of May 2014.[19]

Haiti

The Executive Director of Asosyasyon Fanm Soley Doyiti (AFASDA) stated that about 600 cases of domestic violence were reported out of more than 2,555 cases of violence against women. (22 May 2013). It is generally accepted that violence to women is widespread and sources indicate that 70 per cent of Haitian women have been affected by gender-based violence.

Honduras

Thirty per cent of Honduran women say they have been abused and the murder rate more than doubled in eight years from 2005 through to 2013. According to the University Institute for Democracy, Peace and Security, 636 women were murdered in Honduras in 2013. The figures for 2014 were slightly down to 531 women; the majority killed were aged between 15 and 24.

It is believed that many of the killings are drug- and/or gang-related and the US policy of deporting criminals to the region has made matters worse. The policy has resulted in the combined deportations to Honduras, El Salvador and Guatemala in 2013 of 106,420 persons. The overall statistics show that of 300,000 deportees of these 57 per cent had a criminal conviction.[20] According to an Interpol study, from 1998 to 2009 the homicide rate rose from 24 to 47 in Guatemala, from 30 to 51 in El Salvador, and jumped from 41 to 68 in Honduras.[21]

Jamaica

Although it is generally accepted that domestic violence is a huge and widespread problem in Jamaica there are no official figures to confirm this. Reports suggest that sexual and domestic violence is under-reported because of cultural norms and fear of further violence. The lack of confidence that the police will afford protection is also believed to be responsible for under reporting of domestic violence. The *Jamaica Gleaner* reported that 24 women were killed in 2016 by a partner or former partner an increase on the 15 women murdered in 2015.[22]

Mexico

A 2013 study by the National Commission for Prevention and Eradication of violence against women (Conavim) reports 66 per cent of all Mexican women 15 and older have suffered abuse. The Mexican Government has put the figure higher, at 80 per cent of women abused. According to the UN, Mexico is considered one of the world's 20 worst countries when it comes to violence against women. "Violence against women isn't an epidemic, it's a pandemic in Mexico," said Ana Guezmez, Mexico's representative for United Nations Women. "We still don't see it as a central theme of the current administration. You have to send a much stronger message."[23]

In the State of Mexico alone, more than 2,300 women have been killed over a nine-year period according to The National Citizen Femicide Observatory. According to the observatory, six women are killed every day. Of the 3,892 femicides identified in 2012-13 only 24 per cent were investigated by the authorities and only 1.6 per cent led to sentencing.[24] Mexico has an overall homicide rate of 22 murders per 100,000 people per year. Some cities are worse than others. Five of the 10 most violent cities in Latin America are in Mexico: Acapulco, Ciudad Juárez, Torreón, Chihuahua, and Durango.

Not all of Mexico is unsafe, as Harvard scholar Viridiana Ríos has pointed out; the illegal drug cartels run their violent operations in less than one-third of all Mexican municipal districts. The carnage is concentrated: more than eight of 10 homicides in Mexico take place in contested cartel zones along the border and in the states of Sinaloa and Guerrero. The US-Mexico border has long been a dangerous place for women. More than one-fifth of the women killed in Mexico in 2012 were slain in three of the four states neighbouring Texas, according to the national statistics agency. None of the figures include the many women who have gone missing or those corpses so badly mutilated that authorities cannot even identify their gender.

Human rights groups say security forces are often involved in sexual abuse and disappearance of women. About 4,000 women disappeared in Mexico in 2011-12, mostly in Chihuahua (where hundreds of women were murdered or kidnapped in the 1990s), and the State of Mexico, according to the National Observatory Against Femicide. With 22.7 murders for every 100,000 women in 2012, Chihuahua is still Mexico's most dangerous state for women.

In Mexico City so many teenage girls turned up dead in a vacant field on the outskirts of the city that people nicknamed it the "women's dumping ground". Bodies began showing up in 2006, usually left among piles of garbage. Some were victims of domestic violence, others of drug gangs that seized control of entire neighbourhoods, imposing their will on residents and feeding a culture of extreme violence. Although the dumping ground has since been cleared and declared an ecological reserve, its grisly past is not forgotten and the killings continue.

Montserrat

There are no research figures for domestic violence on Montserrat, but the Deputy Commissioner for the Royal Montserrat Police Force reported that "threats of violence" had been the most frequently reported incident to the police since 2007. The Montserrat Women's Centre said there is a desperate need for laws to protect women and girls from and provide recourse for damages such as physical, sexual, emotional and personal abuse, sexual harassment at work, at school and on the streets.

Nicaragua

Domestic violence is widespread in Nicaragua; according to police figures 34.5 per cent of all crimes reported last year involved domestic violence. Every 20 minutes a Nicaraguan woman or girl falls victim to domestic violence or sexual abuse, according to Nicaragua's country representative for UNICEF, who says that 29 per cent of Nicaraguan women are victims of sexual violence or domestic violence despite its campaign "Let's unite for a life without violence, no more victims".

Panama

Domestic violence against women is a serious problem in Panama, with few convictions for killers, who are often convicted of "unintentional killing" in cases of abuse that led to death. Figures from Panama's Public Defender's Office show that the number of reported femicides nearly doubled from 42 in 2008 to 80 in 2009, with the highest percentage being committed by firearms in the province of Panama.

According to figures from the National System of Criminal Statistics System (SIEC), in the first five months of 2015 domestic violence in Panama increased by 12 per cent: 8,747 complaints were made, as compared to 7,199 complaints in the same period in 2014.[25]

Paraguay

Although the law criminalizes spousal abuse, it stipulates that the abuse must be habitual before being recognized as criminal, and then is punishable by a fine. Between January and August 2006, the Secretariat of Women's Affairs recorded 1,004 cases of domestic violence. Despite an apparent trend toward increased reporting of complaints, such complaints were often withdrawn soon after filing due to spousal reconciliation or family pressure, including from the attacker, who is often the spouse.

Peru
A survey published by Peru's National Institute of Statistics and Information (INEI) shows that more than one in three women have experienced domestic violence. An INEI survey carried out in 2012 revealed that 37 per cent of women aged 15-49 have been victimised by a spouse or partner. In some of the highlands, the prevalence of domestic violence rose about 50 per cent.

Puerto Rico
According to official figures 20,000 cases of domestic violence are recorded every year but activists point out that the figure is likely to be much higher, as many cases of domestic violence go unreported. The America Civil Liberties Union (ACLU) reported that Puerto Rico has the highest per capita rate in the world for women over 14 who are killed by their intimate partner: 107 women were killed by their intimate partner in the five-year period 2007 to 2011. The numbers increased significantly to 30 women killed in 2011. That year the number of women killed in Puerto Rico was six times higher than in Los Angeles, which has about the same population of about 3.7 million.[26]

Saint Kitts and Nevis
Violence against women continues to be a "serious and pervasive problem" as the government reported that in 2010 there were 245 cases of domestic violence recorded. There were also 111 requests for protection orders, of which 68 were granted. In 2012 there were 104 requests for protection orders, of which 43 were granted. The Ministry of Gender Affairs obtained 51 convictions for domestic violence out of the 78 cases they submitted from the 197 complaints they recorded.[27]

Saint Lucia

Although no figures on the prevalence of domestic violence in St Lucia could be found it is widely believed to be significant. The Minister for Gender Relations is reported to have said that violence to women is a "major challenge"[28] The Saint Lucian delegate to the Caribbean Association for Feminist Research and Action (CAFRA) in July 2006, described domestic violence in St Lucia as "a crisis situation" and stated that "at least" five women had been killed so far in 2006 due to domestic violence.[29]

Saint Vincent and the Grenadines

Domestic and sexual violence are "serious and pervasive" and among the "most serious human rights problems" in St Vincent and the Grenadines.[30] According to the United Nations Office on Drugs and Crime Report in 2007 St Vincent had the world's third highest rate of domestic violence. There were 168 cases of sexual violence in 2010 and 426 in 2011. The rate of sexual violence was 154 cases per 100,000 people in 2010, rising to 389 cases per 100,000 in 2011.

Suriname

Violence against women was a common problem. The Ministry of Justice and police registered 1, 213 cases of domestic violence during 2010, a drop from 1,769 in 2009. The UN reported that in 2010 at least 11.7 per cent of Surinamese women self-reported that they experienced domestic violence in their households. General crime figures show a murder rate of 6.1 per 100.000 people, a rate lower than most in the region.

Trinidad and Tobago

Data from the Crime and Problem Analysis (CAPA) branch of the Trinidad and Tobago Police Services (TTPS) recorded that there were approximately 11,441 cases of domestic violence related incidents reported between 2010 and 2015. Approximately 75 per cent of the cases were female. During the same period there were 131 domestic violence related deaths, of which 56 per cent were women.

The *Trinidad Express* reported that "Domestic violence against women has reached "epidemic" levels in Trinidad and Tobago with more than 10,000 women seeking restraining orders every year.... Between the period 1991 and 2014 more than 125, 000 applications for protection orders were filed in the courts. In 2005 alone the police responded to 1,613 reports of domestic violence. 1,238 of those reports were made by women".[31]

Turks and Caicos Islands

No official records on domestic violence could be found for the Turks and Caicos Islands but the Head of the Sexual offences and domestic violence Unit said that domestic violence and sexual offences are the most common cause of injury to women and children in the Islands.[32]

United States of America

Figures released by the US Department of Justice on 5 September 2014 show:

- Women who have experienced domestic violence: 25 per cent
- Number of children who witness domestic violence annually: 6 million
- Estimated number of domestic violence incidents every year: 960,000
- Percentage of men who are victims of domestic violence: 15%
- The health costs for domestic violence annually: $5.8 billion
- Number of women killed by husbands or boyfriends each day: 2

Family violence costs to the nation in medical expenses, police and court costs, shelter and foster care, sick leave, absenteeism and non-productivity $7.5 billion annually.

In addition, the Centre of Disease Control and Prevention say every minute 20 persons are victims of domestic violence in the USA.

US Virgin Islands

No figures for domestic violence in the US Virgin Islands could be found but there are reports of at least two domestic violence projects on the Islands. News that the former Police Captain was found guilty of second-degree murder and other felony charges stemming from the violent death of his wife drew a response from Government House: "This is a tragic moment stemming from the scourge of domestic violence. It is a plague haunting many families," said the Governor Mr Kenneth Mapp.[33]

Uruguay
Statistics show the rate of femicide in Uruguay, with a population of 3.3 million, to be significantly higher than in other South American countries. A wide variety of civil society organizations that were part of an IACHR hearing on 25 October 2010 contend that the mistreatment of women by the Uruguayan legal system has allowed rampant domestic violence and femicide to persist.

Venezuela
The Public Defence Ministry received 59,876 claims for domestic violence from January to October 2015 through the 68 specialised legal offices in the country. Although there are no government figures for domestic violence available, it is widely accepted that it is a "common problem" with reports suggesting only 10 per cent of cases are ever reported because it is often seen as a "private" issue. Venezuela has one of the highest murder rates in the world; with every other person owning a gun it comes as no surprise.

Scale of violence in the Americas.
Latin America has a higher than average incidence of domestic violence with UN figures showing 35 per cent of women experiencing domestic violence worldwide; the average in the Americas is likely closer to 50 per cent abused, with some countries recording well above that figure. Of the 25 countries in the world that are "high" or "very high" in the UN rankings for femicide, more than half are in Latin America, with El Salvador topping the list. Reliable figures for domestic violence are hard to come by as many governments in the region do not keep adequate records. Many women will have life-changing injuries and some will live daily in fear of abuse. Some 40 per cent of Brazilian women who have been abused report that domestic violence rarely happens, but 20 per cent report it as a daily occurrence.

Domestic violence figures are generally unreliable as estimates of 40 per cent not reporting are common and likely to be on the conservative side. Figures can fluctuate wildly but the general trend for violence seems to be an upward one, unfortunately. Some of the increase is as a result of more awareness about domestic violence but there can be no doubting an actual increase in violence on the whole.

The table below is incomplete because of lack of figures for domestic violence and should be viewed as a rough guide only. The figures used are from government sources, newspaper reports, women's organizations, US Country Reports, UN reports and WHO reports.

Monitoring the crime statistics of a country is important; according to the United Nations Office on Drugs and Crime (UNODC):

"there is a clear link between violent crime and development: crime hampers poor human and economic development; this in turn fosters crime. Improvement to social and economic conditions go hand in hand with the reduction of violent crime."

Generally the countries with the lowest rankings of GDP per capita are the ones with the highest murder rates. Of the 25 most murderous countries in the world 18 are located in the Americas, with Honduras, El Salvador and Venezuela topping the list in that order.

HOMICIDE STATISTICS FOR THE AMERICAS

Country	Homicides	TOTAL Homicide Rate per 100,000	% of Victims male	MALE Homicides	Homicide Rate	FEMALE % of victims female	Homicides	Homicides Rate	Year of ratio data
Antigua &Barbuda	10 5	11.2	67.9%	7	7.6	32.1%	3	3.6	2011 2015
Argentina	2,237 2,837	5.5 6.6	83.6%	1,870	4.6	16.4 %	367 235	0.9	2011 2015
Bahamas	111 146	29.8 37.0	87.4%	97	26.0	12.0%	14	3.8	2011 2015
Barbados	21 31	7.4 11.3	67.7%	14	5.0	32.3 %	7	2.4	2010 2015
Belize	145 119	44.7 40	90.3%	131	40.4	9.7%	14	4.3	2011 2015
Bolivia	1,270	12.1 10.8	77.3%	982	9.4	22.7%	288	2.7	2012 2016
Brazil	50,108 52,463	25.2	89.8% 25.7	44,997	22.6	10.2%	5,111 4,762	2.6 4.8	2010 2015
Cayman Islands	8	14.7	87.5%	7	12.9	12.5%	1	1.8	2010
Chile	550	3.1 3.6	81.9	450	2.5	18.1%	100	0.6	2010 2014

HOMICIDE STATISTICS FOR THE AMERICAS

Country	TOTAL			MALE		FEMALE			Year of ratio data
	Homicides	Homicide Rate per 100,000	% of Victims male	Homicides	Homicide Rate	% of victims female	Homicides	Homicide Rate	
Colombia	14,670	30.8 37	91.6%	13,438	28.2	8.4%	1,232	2.6	2012 2016
Costa Rica	407 577	8.5 11.8	87.7 %	357	7.5	12.3	50	1.0	2011 2016
Cuba	477	4.2	75.0%	358	3.2	25.0%	119	1.1	2012
Dominica	15 12	21.1 22	8.75%	13	18.5	12.5%	2	2.6	2010 2015
Dominican Republic	2,268	22.1 25.	91.1%	2,066	20.1	8.9%	202	2.0	2010 2016
Ecuador	1,924 914	12.4 5.6	91.8%	1,766	11.4	8.2%	158	1.0	2010 2016
El Salvador	2,594 5,278	41.2 81.2	89.0%	2,309	36.7	11.0%	285	4.5	2010 2016
French Guiana	30	13.3	81.8%	25	10.9	18.2%	5	2.4	2012
Grenada	14	13.3	64.3%	9	8.6	35.7%	5	4.7	2010

HOMICIDE STATISTICS FOR THE AMERICAS

Country	TOTAL			MALE		FEMALE			Year of ratio data
	Homicides	Homicide Rate per 100,000	% of Victims male	Homicides	Homicide Rate	% of victims female	Homicides	Homicides Rate	
Guadeloupe	36	7.9	84.2%	30	6.7	15.8%	6	1.2	2011
Guatemala	6,025 / 4,520	39.9 / 27.3	88.9%	5,356	35.5	11.1%	669	4.4	2011 / 2016
Guyana	139 / 135	18.4 / 17	60.0%	81	10.2	40.0%	54	6.8	2010 / 2012
Haiti	1,033	10.2	78.4%	810	8.0	21.6%	223	2.2	2012
Honduras	7,172 / 5,154	90.4 / 59	93.2%	6,684	84.3	6.8%	488	6.1	2010 / 2016
Jamaica	1,087 / 1,350	39.3 / 50	89.5%	973	35.2	10.5%	114	4.1	2010 / 2016
Martinique	11	2.7	72.7%	8	2.0	27.3%	3	0.7	2010
Mexico	26,037 / 20,858	21.5 / 16.2	89.3%	23,251	19.2	10.7%	2,786	2.3	2012 / 2016
Montserrat	1	20.4	100.0%	1	20.4	0.0%	0	0.0	2010

HOMICIDE STATISTICS FOR THE AMERICAS

Country	TOTAL			MALE		FEMALE			Year of ratio data
	Homicides	Homicide Rate per 100,000	% of Victims male	Homicides	Homicide Rate	% of victims female	Homicides	Homicides Rate	
Nicaragua	675 460	11.3 7	92.6%	625	10.5	7.4%	50	0.8	2010 2016
Panama	654 375	7.2 9.3	94.6%	619	16.3	5.4%	35	0.9	2009 2016
Paraguay	649 617	9.7 8.8	88.8%	576	8.6	11.2%	73	1.1	2009 2016
Peru	2,865	9.6 7.2	78.1%	2,238	7.5	21.9%	627	2.1	2010 2015
Puerto Rico	978 679	26.5 20	94.1%	926	24.9	5.9%	58	1.6	2010 2016
St Kitts and Nevis	18 27	33.6 38	90.5%	16	30.4	9.5%	2	3.2	2011 2015
St Lucia	39 28	21.6 25	79.7%	31	17.2	20.36%	8	4.4	2008 2015
St Vincent	28 24	25.6 22	88.0%	25	22.5	12.03%	3	3.1	2010 2015
Suriname	33	6.1	75.3%	25	4.6	24.7%	8	1.5	2010

HOMICIDE STATISTICS FOR THE AMERICAS

Country	TOTAL			MALE		FEMALE			Year of ratio data
	Homicides	Homicide Rate per 100,000	% of Victims male	Homicides	Homicide Rate	% of victims female	Homicides	Homicides Rate	
Trinidad and Tobago	379 463	28.3 35	91.7%	348	26.0%	8.3%	31	2.3	2010 2016
Turks and Caicos	2	6.6	100.0%	2	6.6	0.0%	0	0.0	2010
USA	14,827 15,696	4.7	77.8%	11,535	3.7	22.2%	3,292	1.0	2010 2015
US Virgin Islands	56	52.6 32.9	87.5%	49	46.0	12.5%	7	6.6	2010 2015
Uruguay	267 265	7.9 7.6	79.4%	212	6.3	20.6%	55	1.6	2010 2016
Venezuela	16,072 21,752	53.7 70.1	91.9%	14,770	49.4	8.1%	1,302	43	2010 2016

Notes to Chapter 7

1   *The Buenos Aires Herald*, 25 November 2016.
2   Heather Sutton, "Crime and violence in the Bahamas". IDB series on Crime and Violence in the Caribbean. 2016.
3   *Belize Times*, 12 May 2011.
4   Leanne McGrath, "Domestic violence increase warning", *The Royal Castle*, 11 July 2014.
5   Al-Jazeera, 28 July 2016
6   Lisa Nikolau, "Activists: Bolivia needs to do more to stop killings, violence against women", *Humanosphere*, 4 January 2017.
7   Talita Nascimento, "Violence against women in Brazil: it is time to break the silence", *Brazil Talk*, 8 March 2016.
8   Brent Fuller, "Crime Stats: Burglaries down, gun crimes up", *Cayman Compass*, 24 February 2017.
9   L. Arias, "Costa Rica sees rise in domestic violence", *The Tico Times*, 13 April 2016.
10   Patricia Grogg, *Havana Times*, 25 May 2009.
11   Daily news *Dominican Today*, November 2011.
12   Liz Scherffius, "Ecuador Initiates Campaign to Prevent Violence against Women", Telesur News, 27/12/2016.
13   US Department of State's Country Reports on Human Rights Protection for 2014.
14   UN Special Rapporteur on Violence, 14 February 2011, para 18.
15   Al Jazeera, 7 June 2013.
16   News Agency Inter Press Service (IPS), 10 April 2013.
17   UN report, 14 February 2011, para 21.
18   Laurent Borredon, "Crime and unemployment dog Guadeloupe", *The Guardian*, 27 December 2011 (originally appeared in *La Monde*).
19   "Murder Rate Climbs to 74", *Kaieteur News*, 13 June 2015.
20   Al Jazeera, 9 September 2014.
21   Interpol study published 27 February 2014.
22   Nadine Wilson-Harris, "Shame! –Twenty-four women killed in 2016", *Jamaica Gleaner*, 18 December 2016.
23   CCTV America, 20 September 2015.
24   "Women in Mexico rally against rampant domestic violence", Al Jazeera,
21   July 2015.
25   News Room Panama. "Panama domestic violence up – homicides down", posted 12 July 2015.
26   American Civil Liberties Union website 2017.
27   United States Department of State Country Report 2016
28   *The Voice*, 8 November 2014.
29   Caribbean Media Corporation, July 2006
30   The US Department of State's Country Reports on Human Rights Protection 2012.
31   Camille Hunt, *Trinidad Express,* 6 December 2016.
32   *Turks and Caicos Weekly News*, pp. 3721-127.htm.
33 The Virgin Island Consortium, 27 March 2017.

Chapter 8

THE STATE'S RESPONSE TO DOMESTIC VIOLENCE

Appreciating the size of the problem and learning from the measures taken by governments in the region to combat domestic violence are essential in advancing best practice. Figures for domestic violence are often conservative estimates, because most incidents of abuse go unreported. The aim here is not to give comprehensive coverage of the laws and actions taken by governments, but to provide example of the action taken. For those looking for more detailed and up-to-date information, these can best be gleaned from government websites.

Despite most Latin American countries' representatives attending the domestic violence conference in Brazil and signing the 1994 Convention of Belém, requiring them to educate their people about women's rights, fight machismo and pass laws to protect women, the incidence of domestic violence against women continues to spiral out of control across the region.

According to ECLAC, 20 countries in Latin America and the Caribbean now have laws against domestic violence although only eight have earmarked specific funds in their national Budget for the issue; 14 countries have a separate criminal classification for femicide – gender-motivated murders. There has to be renewed and ongoing efforts to end domestic violence. Let us look at the efforts to combat domestic violence made by some of the countries in the region thus far, while bearing in mind that new projects start and others fail.

Antigua and Barbuda

A Domestic Violence Bill 2015 was enacted by the parliament of Antigua and Barbuda "to provide greater protection for victims of domestic violence and to make provision for the granting of protection orders and for matters incidental thereto and connected therewith."

The bill gives a detailed definition of domestic violence and gives the police powers to arrest a person at the scene of a domestic violence incident without a warrant. The Court can make an Order directing police officers to seize any firearm or dangerous weapon in possession of a respondent.

Argentina

The provincial Cordoba Legislature passed its first domestic violence law in March 2006. The legislation is quite inclusive. The term "family" takes in fiancées and former or current common-law husbands or wives. The law also defines domestic violence as physical, psychological and economic violence. The law prohibits domestic violence and provides for removal of the abusive spouse from the home; but it does not provide penalties unless the violence involves crimes against "sexual integrity". In this case penalties can be as much as 20 years' imprisonment.

Any person suffering physical or psychological domestic violence may file a formal complaint with a judge or police station. The law gives family court judges the right to prevent the perpetrator of a violent act from entering the victim's home or workplace. Charges also may be brought in a criminal court, which may apply corresponding penalties.

In March 2006, the Interior Ministry launched a federal programme that included creating a mobile unit for providing assistance to victims of sexual and domestic violence. The programme was to have a national reach, with its initial implementation in late October 2006 in the city of Buenos Aires, with two mobile units working 24 hours a day. Each unit, composed of a psychologist a social worker, and two police officials attend whenever they receive complaints of domestic violence.

In December 2006, the Buenos Aires Supreme Court ordered the criminal, family and minors' courts, as well as provincial courts in civil and family matters, to have duty officers to receive complaints of domestic violence and assist victims after normal court hours. Victims could call a cell phone number to get assistance.

The Buenos Aires municipal government operated a small shelter for battered women and a 24-hour hotline offering support and guidance to victims of violence. Public and private institutions also offer prevention programmes and provide support and treatment for abused women.

The Argentine President, Mauricio Macri, announced in July 2016 a National Plan to fight violence against women. He said: "education was the key to ending deeply rooted cultural patterns of violence." The Plan is scheduled to start in 2017 and includes creating a network of women refuges and money for electronic tagging of violent men. In presenting the Plan the president said: "We all need to commit ourselves. This is not only the job of government it is for society too." The President of the National Council of Women, a government agency, said the Plan would last three years and that it includes introducing gender awareness in the school curriculum and increased staffing at a telephone helpline for women.[1]

Bahamas

The Domestic Violence (Probation Orders) Act commenced 1 December 2008 "to provide for the granting of Probation orders in circumstances surrounding domestic violence and for related and consequential matters". The Act provides a definition of domestic violence that includes physical, sexual, emotional, psychological and financial abuse. The law provides for the granting of protection orders by the courts, the breaking of which can incur penalties of a fine of $5,000, or 12 months' imprisonment, or both. It requires for the police to provide protection and information to the victim when attending a scene of domestic violence. The officer must make a written report of the incident to be kept on record by the officer in charge of the station. The Ministry for social security has responsibility to raise awareness about domestic violence, provide shelters and counselling for victims and developing educational programmes for the prevention of domestic violence and for the rehabilitation of perpetrators.

Barbados

The Domestic Violence (Protection Orders) Act of 1993 provides for the granting of protection orders in domestic violence and related matters, and provides for a magistrate to grant a protection order that:

- prohibits abuse and molestation
- excludes the abusive person from the home or workplace
- gives the applicant the right to occupy the home
- provides for the use of furniture and household effects, payment of rent utilities, etc.

Under a new Domestic Violence(Prevention Order)(Amendment) Bill 2016, a junior police officer may issue an emergency protection order if he or she has reason to believe that such an order is necessary to ensure the safety of a person at risk. Low-ranking officers may also issue emergency protection orders without the consent of the persons at risk. It also gives the Royal Barbados Police Force authority to enter any premises without a warrant if an officer has reasonable grounds to suspect that an emergency protection order, an interim protection order or a final protection order is being breached. Officers will be given the power to enter premises – upon the invitation of a person resident there or independently – if there is reasonable grounds to suspect that a person on the premises has suffered, or is in imminent danger of suffering, physical injury at the hands of some other person.

Belize

In 2010, the government released its National Gender-Based Violence Plan of Action for 2010-13. It was issued by the Women's Department and strategies adopted are predicated on the findings of The National Assessment of Actions on Ending Violence against Women (2009), which sets out the Belize framework for actions on violence against women, including international commitments, national policies, laws and legislative reform. The Assessment also gives a set of guiding principles for work in this area, and sets out 43 recommendations in the areas of Understanding Violence and Raising Awareness.

Additional measures for addressing domestic violence include the Women's Department, which has a Domestic Violence Task Force and a Family Violence Committee. All districts of the country have Women Development Officers. The Women's Department uses the Gender-Based Violence Registration Form to track the incidence of Gender-Based Violence. The form is intended to document the first point of contact the client has with one of the agencies involved in rendering assistance to victims of gender-based violence.

Government services directed at victims include Community Counselling Centres, a Family Violence Unit hotline, operated by the police department and two shelters. The government is also actively involved in training and prevention programming. In 2008, the Women's Department partnered with the Magistrate's Courts in Belize City launched a pilot Batterer's Intervention Program. Defendants in domestic abuse cases are referred from the Magistrate's Court and the Family Court. The first cycle of the 16-week psycho-educational programme was completed in July 2010.

The Women's Department of the Ministry of Human Development and Social Transformation also conducts training on domestic and gender-based violence for police officers, police prosecutors, magistrates, community nurses, social workers, education professionals, religious and community leaders, schools and communities.

The Gender Awareness Safe School Program was implemented in one primary and one secondary school per district per school year. The issue of violence against women and gender equality was included in this programme. In 2006, the Ministry of Education organized training for high school teachers, based on the Teaching Guide developed for this programme by the Women's Department. A new comprehensive domestic violence law was passed in 2013, outlawing many forms of abuse of women, including marital rape.

Bermuda

The Domestic Violence (Protection Orders) Act 1997 and the Stalking Act 1997 are intended to afford protection to victims of domestic violence. The Acts make provision for Protection

Orders where there is a demonstrated instance of abuse or the threat of violence or abuse. Breaking the conditions of the Protection Orders can lead to arrest and prosecution.

Bolivia

President Evo Morales passed Law 348 in 2013 that sets out to give greater protection to victims of domestic violence. The law allows for special prosecutors and courts for gender-based crimes, shelters for women and makes femicide punishable by 30 years in prison. There has been some criticism about the implementation of the law and the national newspaper *La Razon* reported that since the law was passed there have been 206 cases of femicide with only sentences in eight cases. The overtaxed justice system is often blamed for many women giving up on their cases.

The Justice Minister and the Magistrates Council introduced new measures for fighting domestic violence: to apply for public office Bolivian men must produce a document stating that they have no criminal record of gender violence or violence against a family member.

Brazil

President Lula signed the Law of Domestic and Family Violence on 7 August 2006, and for the first time in Brazil's history domestic violence against women was codified and specifically defined. The Maria da Penha law was passed with the intention of finally meeting the commitments made when Brazil ratified the Convention on the Elimination of All Forms of Discrimination against Women (CEDAW), an international treaty adopted in 1979 by the UN General Assembly. Described as an international bill of rights for women, it was instituted on 3 September 1981 and ratified by 189 countries.

The Law defines the commitments of government to develop public policies and guidelines aimed at ensuring the human rights of women, within the household and family relations, through a co-ordinated set of actions by the Federal State, the Federal District, the municipalities and non-governmental entities. It seeks to implement the changes by strengthening multidisciplinary networks, including legal aid for victims, specialised police assistance, psychological support, law enforcement, social services, health, education, work, and housing. In addition, the law allows for the creation of special courts for domestic and family violence against women in all Brazilian states. It amends the criminal code and triples previous punishments for those convicted of such crimes and allows for the possibility of preventive imprisonment. Brazil's law on violence against women is widely seen as exemplary but activists argue that the laws have made little difference to the levels of violence.

Cayman Islands
The Cayman Islands first enacted the Summary Jurisdiction (Domestic Violence) Law in 1992. It was revised in 1998 and new legislation of 2010 provides "added protection for a wider range of victims and potential victims", guiding those who work to assist them and enabling more effective prosecution of perpetrators. The new law broadens the definition of domestic violence to include actions that may be considered to cause or intended to cause financial, emotional, psychological or sexual abuse. It expands the definition of those afforded protection to include legal spouses, men and women living together as husband or wife, a child of the family, a parent, a man and woman who are or have been in a visiting relationship and a dependant of the alleged abuser who is living in the household. It increases the type of court orders available, including protection orders, occupancy orders, tenancy orders and ancillary orders.

New aspects of the law include:

• The breaching of any court order can incur a fine of $10,000 or imprisonment of up to two years or both.
• The court may order the victim or perpetrator or both to participate in appropriate treatment or counselling programme.

Chile
As recently as 1989 the Civil Code of Chile legally sanctioned husbands' complete ownership and authority over their wives. The Inter-Family Violence Law passed in 1994 was the first

domestic violence law for Chile. Under Michelle Bachelet, the first woman President of Chile, many advances were made from 2006 to 2010. She increased the budget for Chilean National Ministry for Women (SERNAM) and secured funding from the UN for many projects. By the end of 2006 there were 29 government and private centres for the victims of domestic violence. SERNAM and NGOs combined to provide training on legal, medical, and psychological effects of domestic violence for the police, judicial and municipal authorities.

Colombia

Colombia has made important progress in constructing a legal and policy framework to protect women and girls from gender-based violence and to promote the rights to health and justice for survivors. Although some gaps in legal protections remain, Congress passed some of the most comprehensive legislation on violence against women in the region in 2008. The same year, the Constitutional Court ordered various ministries to address gender-based violence against displaced women and girls. In 2011, the government issued regulations to implement the laws and court orders, and developed a comprehensive "referral pathway" to ensure that service providers can guide victims of gender-based violence to all of the services available, including health services, justice, protection, and psycho-social support. In addition, the Colombia Ombudsman's Office of Human Rights conducted regional training workshops: to promote the application of domestic violence statutes, to provide a clear, inter-ministerial plan for implementing the measures of prevention and punishment of violence against women and protection and care of victims. The government also passed the Law Against Femicide No 1761 of 6 July 2015.

Colombia's chief advisor on gender equality, Cristina Plazas, puts much of the blame on Colombia's macho culture: "One of the main reasons behind violence against women in Colombia, and the rest of Latin America, is machismo. Some men think that to be a man they have to control women and believe women have to be at home looking after children and doing the housework."[2]

Domestic violence in Colombia remains a serious problem, despite judicial authorities having power to remove abusers from the household and require therapy or re-education of them; perpetrators also face prison time if the abuse causes grave harm or the abuse is recurrent.

Costa Rica
The Law against Domestic Violence was enacted in 1996 and allows several measures including:

- Protective measures can be enforced without recourse to criminal or civil proceedings.
- The perpetrator of physical, sexual or psychological violence can be removed from the home and denied access to the survivor.
- Perpetrators can be temporarily barred from access to under-aged children.
- Perpetrators weapons can be confiscated.
- Perpetrators can be forced to pay maintenance of the family and any damage caused to property.

Cuba
There are no specific domestic violence laws in Cuba so it is not surprising that there are no recorded figures for this crime. The government often refers to several Articles of the constitution, the penal code and other legislation promoting gender equality when challenged about protection for victims of domestic violence. The government may be in some denial about domestic violence but activists are determined to get it on the agenda and have begun campaigning for change in Cuba.

Dominica
The Protection against Domestic Violence Act 2001 affords injunctive relief to victims of domestic violence in the form of protection, occupation and tenancy orders from the courts. The Act allows for perpetrators of domestic violence to be prevented from entering or remaining on the premises of the survivor. The Act also allows police to enter a premises without a warrant where domestic violent is suspected.

Dominican Republic

Article 42 of the constitution condemns domestic violence and the law makes it a criminal offence. The state can prosecute rape, incest, sexual aggression and other forms of domestic violence. Penalties for the crimes range from one to 40 years imprisonment with fines from 700 to 245,000 pesos.

The amended Penal Code penalises domestic violence with four to 10 years in prison and a significant fine. If the victim is incapacitated for more than 90 days the sentence is 10- 20 years. Those causing permanent injury or damage face a maximum 30 years' imprisonment.

The law provides for protection Orders with a number of sanctions, including:

- Orders to refrain from molesting, incarcerating or threatening a spouse, ex-spouse, partner, ex-partner, or consensual partner...
- order to evict the aggressor from the residence of a spouse, ex-spouse, partner ex-partner, or consensual partner
- forbidding the victim to hide children they may have in common or move them elsewhere.

The Ministry of Women runs a number of shelters for the victims of domestic violence and their children; they also run a 24-hour emergency hotline for the victims of abuse.

Ecuador

Ecuador is one of the leading countries on the rights of women in the region. In 1929 Ecuadorian women were the first to vote in the region. The Law Against Violence to Women was enacted in 1995 and it aims to "protect the physical and mental integrity and sexual freedom of women and members of their families by preventing and punishing domestic violence and other violations of women and their families. The Law provides for protective measures including:

- Ordering that an assailant be removed from the home.
- Prohibiting the assailant from coming into contact with or approaching the victim

- preventing the assailant from intimidating the victim or the victim's family
- ordering the parties including minors to undergo therapy.

The Constitution was rewritten in 1998 specifying equal rights for men and women in numerous areas. They established in 1981 the first police stations run by women for Women and Families, which handle issues including domestic violence. The government's National Commission on Women (CONAMU) may accept complaints about abuse of women but must refer cases to the prosecutor's office for action. Women may file complaints against a rapist or an abusive spouse or companion but only if they produce a witness. CONAMU has projects in all provinces, focusing primarily on equal opportunities, public policy programmes toward women, and lines of credit for women's businesses. In some police stations, social workers employed by city governments or NGOs assist victims with legal and psychological support. They also offer legal and psychological services to victims of violence in most provinces.

El Salvador

The Law against Domestic Violence was enacted in 1996 and modified in 2013. Article 3 of the Law defines domestic violence as "any act or omission, direct or indirect that causes harm, physical, sexual, or psychological suffering, or death to members of the family." Article 200 of the criminal code prohibits domestic violence and provides for sentences from one to three years of imprisonment.

Article 7 of the Law against Domestic Violence includes provisions for different forms of protection available to victims, including court orders. Article 10 includes provisions on measures that the police must take, including providing the victim with information and issuing temporary protection measures for up to 48 hours.

Family courts also have the power to remove an abusive spouse from the home if continued cohabitation creates a risk to the victim. The courts may issue restraining orders prohibiting the abusive spouse from approaching the victim or her place of employment or study; prohibiting the abusive spouse from persecuting or intimidating the victim or any member of her family; reinserting the victim into the family home, if shared, while simultaneously removing the abusive spouse from the premises; and ordering any treatment deemed beneficial to the affected family.

However, there has been considerable criticism of the law and its implementation. The Director of Centre for Gender and Refugee Studies (CGRS) based at the University of California stated that laws against domestic violence are not effectively enforced "due to deep-seated discriminatory norms, inadequate implementation, and insufficient funding"[3]

He has also criticised the way the provision for reconciliation in the Domestic Violence Law was still being used to pressure women into remaining in abusive relationships, despite the Law being abrogated by the Legislative assembly in 2002 as a result of "the widespread abuse" of the provision.[4]

US Country Reports 2014 points out that the law "prohibits mediation in domestic violence disputes", and the principal attorney at Las Dignas similarly said that "formal conciliation procedures" had been repealed under the Law Against Domestic Violence.[5]

At the time of writing there was one state shelter run by the Salvadoran Institute for the Development of Women (Instituto Salvadoreño para el Desarrollo de la Mujer, ISDEMU). The shelter can accommodate 35 women and children victims of domestic violence. According to ISDEMU's website, the shelter provides psychological, medical, legal and social assistance, among other services. In addition, they provide a daily 24-hour free telephone helpline.

French Guiana

French Guiana is an overseas department of France under article 73 of the French Constitution (1958); the laws and regulations of France apply fully and unconditionally in the overseas departments and regions, with adaptations possible to take account of special characteristics.

According to the brochure Conjugal Violence: Legislation is Progressing, published by the Ministry of Social Affairs, Health and Women's Rights, French Legislation "protects all women victims of domestic violence living in France regardless of their nationality or legal status in the country".

Some of the measures contained in Act No 2014-873 of 4 August 2014 for Real Equality Between Men and Women include:

- "the violent spouse must be evicted from the home"
- "strictly limited penal mediation for domestic violence" which is only possible
- "when specifically requested by the victim."

Grenada

A signatory to regional and international conventions and agreements, including CEDAW and Belem do Para, Grenada established a Domestic Violence Unit in 2003 to address the increasing number of incidents. National legislation includes the Domestic Violence Act 2001 and the Child Protection Act 2008. The Unit provides educational material and training in domestic violence awareness to different stakeholders, including for police officers as partners and first responders in the fight against domestic violence. The Domestic Violence Unit also runs a battered women's shelter in the north of the island, staffed with medical and counselling personnel, accommodating about 12 women and their children. A perpetrator programme, "Man -to-Man", provides a 15-week counselling course and men can be court mandated to attend.

The Grenadian House of Representatives approved the Domestic Violence Act of 2010 and implemented it on May 2011 alongside the Domestic Violence and Sexual Assault Protocol. According to the government, the Act includes "stronger tools" for law-enforcement officials, increased penalties for first-time and repeat offenders and greater protection for victims.

Guadeloupe

Guadeloupe is an overseas department of France under article 73 of the French Constitution (1958) the natural laws and regulations of France apply fully and unconditionally in the overseas Departments and regions with adaptations possible to take account of special characteristics.

According to the brochure *Conjugal Violence: Legislation is Progressing*, published by the Ministry of Social Affairs, Health and Women's Rights, French legislation "protects all women victims of domestic violence living in France regardless of their nationality or legal status in the country".

Some of the measures contained in Act No 2014-873 of 4 August 2014 for Real Equality Between Men and Women include:

- "the violent spouse must be evicted from the home"
- "strictly limited penal mediation for domestic violence" which is only possible
- "when specifically requested by the victim."

The website of the prefecture of the region of Guadeloupe states that "the Regional Delegation of Women's Rights and Equality is in charge of implementing in Guadeloupe the Government of France's women's rights Policy, in particular the section on combating violence against women."[6]

Guatemala

The government introduced several new measures to address violence against women and in November 2012, inaugurated a special tribunal to process crimes against women such as sexual violence, trafficking and domestic violence. These tribunals are open 24 hours a day so that women can report violent crimes. It was also announced that 100 new graduates from the National Civil Police had been assigned to work exclusively on crimes of violence against women. It is not known how many of these new officers are women but women's organisations are calling for all police officers to receive training on the application of the new Law against Femicide and other forms of violence against women and on human rights.

The government has been criticised by campaigning groups including Amnesty International for not doing enough; although legislation against domestic violence was introduced in 2008, campaigners claim that very few are held to account for their crimes.

They are concerned about the level of the government's commitment, as it has recently disbanded The National Coordination body to Prevent Violence against Women and Family Violence (CONAPREVI), a state mechanism that had coordinated strategies and dialogued with civil society to end violence. There have also been attacks on the Centres for the Holistic Support of Women Survivors of Violence (CAIMUS,), which were set up by women's organisations and which have supported women survivors of violence for overt 20 years. In 2012 alone they helped 5,000 women. Until recently they were recognised in public policy as a viable alternative, providing holistic support to women and children to protect their security and find solutions to violence.

The CAIMUS implemented a comprehensive care model developed by the Guatemalan Women's Group (GGM), which runs these centres. The model has two strategies: first, women's empowerment, which consists of direct support to women survivors including emergency support, legal advice, psychological support, medical care, temporary refuge and a 24-hour telephone helpline; and secondly, outreach work, which includes setting up support networks for survivors of violence, self-help, security, prevention of violence, awareness raising and training, research and social auditing, advocacy and communication. Despite this, government officials and television personalities have openly criticised the centres and the work of GGM and are calling for the government to stop supporting CAIMUS.

About 20,000 reports of violence against women were made to the police last year; and women's organisations are demanding prosecutions for these crimes. But women who speak out for their rights and against the epidemic of violence in Guatemala are threatened and harassed. Maya Alvarado, from the Guatemalan Women's Union (UNAMG), said that women's organisations are struggling to get their message across: *"Feminism is not well received in Guatemala and we have been called witches in the press, we are not accepted."*

Guyana

The law prohibits domestic violence, gives women the right to seek prompt protection and allows victims to seek occupation, or tenancy orders from a magistrate. Penalties for violation of protection orders include fines up to US$54 (G$10,000) and 12 months' imprisonment. The government uses laws against domestic violence perpetrators with some measure of success. However, there has been some criticism of magistrates and court staff who are often believed to be insensitive to the problem of domestic violence and to their roles in ensuring implementation of the law.

NGOs report a widespread perception that some police officers and magistrates could be bribed to make cases of domestic violence "go away". The government also does not prosecute cases in which the alleged victim or victim's family agree to drop the case in exchange for a monetary payment out of court. NGOs assert the need for a specialized Family Court. Domestic violence is a problem in all regions of the country. Enforcement of the domestic violence laws is especially weak in the interior, where police do not have as strong a presence and courts meet only once a quarter.

Help and Shelter, which is part-funded by donations and some government funding, runs a free shelter for victims of domestic violence and operates a hotline to counsel them. Between January and September 2006 they handled 414 abuse cases, including child, spousal, non-spousal and other domestic abuse; 297 of the cases involved spousal abuse directed against women.

NGOs run public service announcements and train police officers, teachers, nurses, agricultural workers, religious groups, and health clinics to sensitize them to domestic violence. Domestic violence training is part of the curriculum of the Police Training College. A Task Force on Violence against Women includes representatives from NGOs, law-enforcement agencies, the health community and youth.

Haiti

Haitian law prohibits domestic violence against minors but does not classify domestic violence against adults as a distinct crime. The penal code includes penalties for rape but does not address marital rape. Women and girls cannot seek protection orders from judicial officers.

Haiti has only a handful of shelters for domestic violence victims throughout the country, none of which receive government funding. Public health agencies and justice institutions have not been able to agree on a form for documenting forensic evidence or rape, often leaving survivors unable to pursue justice in court even if they make it to a doctor.

According to Country Reports 2012, gender-based violence in Haiti is "committed with near complete impunity" and "the government has yet to implement effective measures to curb the violence, punish perpetrators and provide redress for victims".

Honduras
The Advocates of Human Rights in reviewing Honduras highlighted the pervasiveness of violence against women and the failure of the government to full fill its obligations under the convention to diligently persecute perpetrators of violence and to protect the victims.

The UN special rapporteur against violence to women in Honduras in 2014 noted that "between 2005 and 2013 the number of violent deaths of women rose by 263.4 percent." She added: "statistics from the Public Prosecutors office reflect approximately 16,000 reported allegations of numerous manifestations of violence against women for 2012 with 74.6 percent related to domestic and intra-family violence and 20 percent related to sexual offences."[7]

Jamaica
The government of Jamaica in its Universal Periodic Review to the UN in August 2010 stated that The Domestic Violence (Amendment) Act of 2004 provides for men and women who have been victims of domestic violence to apply for the protection of the courts. This Act broadened the categories of women protected to include not just married women, but also women in common-law and visiting relationships.

In its June 2011 report to the UN Economic and Social Council, the government of Jamaica adds:

This Act continues to be used as a means of redress for women and children. It provides occupation, protection and ancillary orders for victims of domestic violence. The Act also makes special provision for women involved in residential and nonresidential relationships. Proceedings under the Act may now be initiated by a third party on behalf of an abused woman and damage to property has now been recognised as a form of domestic violence.

In its February 2012 report to CEDAW, the Jamaican government specified that "the Bureau of Women's Affairs continues to coordinate and organize sensitizations workshops and seminars for Resident Magistrates and High Court Judges" with over 22 Resident Magistrates and the Office of the Director of Public Prosecutions (DPP) receiving training in how to offer greater redress to women and girls who are victims of violence.

The Bureau of Women's Affairs (BWA) submitted to Parliament a draft National Plan of Action on Violence against Women and Gender-Based Violence. However, in its June 2013 report, the UN Economic, Social and Cultural Rights Committee expressed "its profound concern" at the Jamaican government's "lack of a comprehensive strategy" targeting domestic and sexual violence.

Martinique

Martinique is an overseas department of France under article 73 of the French Constitution (1958) the natural laws and regulations of France apply fully and unconditionally in the overseas Departments and regions with adaptations possible to take account of special characteristics.

According to the brochure *Conjugal Violence: Legislation is Progressing*, published by the Ministry of Social Affairs, Health and Women's Rights, French legislation "protects all women victims of domestic violence living in France regardless of their nationality or legal status in the country".

Some of the measures contained in Act No 2014-873 of 4 August 2014 for Real Equality Between Men and Women include:

- "the violent spouse must be evicted from the home"
- "strictly limited penal mediation for domestic violence", which is only possible
- "when specifically requested by the victim."

Mexico

International pressure over a tide of killings persuaded Mexican lawmakers in 2007 to approve new legislation aimed at preventing violence against women. The new law created a national body to prevent the killings, and urged judges to sign protective orders for abuse victims. The law also established so-called gender violence alerts, a tool to mobilize national, state and local governments to catch perpetrators and reduce murders that has yet to be activated.

The government of Mexico committed to review and consolidate its programme for the prevention, punishment and elimination of violence against women, while giving a voice to civil society and different sectors. Specifically, the Government pledged to: launch permanent campaigns, by means of billboards, travelling expositions, plaques, posters, leaflets and other means of communication; Action Protocols for the Investigation of Crimes Against Women; set up Justice Centres for Women, as a space where different government bodies are represented with the aim of providing comprehensive services (social, educational, health, labour, legal, psychological, immigration, among others) to women in situations of violence, and to guarantee allocation of budget with a gender perspective, so as to ensure a life free of violence for women.

Montserrat

The Family (Protection against Domestic Violence) Act of 24 November 1998 was revised and passed in January 2002 to "Provide Protection in Cases Involving Domestic Violence and for Matters committed therewith". The Act provides for several measures granting protection to the victims of domestic violence including:

• Protection Orders; which could be made to a court to prohibit the respondent from entering or remaining in the household resident of any prescribed person; from attending their place of work or education; from molesting the said person.

Breach of Protection order may result in a $5,000 fine or up to six months in prison or both.

- Occupancy Orders; applications can be made to the court for grant of Occupancy Order, granting the person named in the order the right to live in the household residence.
- Tenancy orders.
- Counselling. The court may recommend either or both parties to participate in counselling of such nature as the court may specify.

Nicaragua

The government recognises domestic violence as a serious and pervasive social and public health problem supported by deeply held cultural norms that condones the use of violence and encourage women to submit to their partners' authority. The government and grass roots organisations are trying to change prevailing attitudes towards violence. Over 100 centres have been set up throughout the country to provide support to battered women or to carry out educational or violence prevention programmes. The majority of the centres are run by local women's organisations who coordinate their actions through a broad based coalition called the National Network of Women against Violence. The Network organises yearly media campaigns and in 1998 successfully lobbied to pass new legislation to protect victims of domestic violence. The Nicaraguan government has also recently initiated a series of programmes to tackle domestic violence, including the introduction of 18 Women and Children's Police Stations in Nicaragua's major cities.

Lawmakers in Nicaragua voted by a huge majority to allow mediation in some cases involving violence against women, while emphasising that women do not have to accept the offer of mediation. Lawmakers from different political parties, the Catholic Church and evangelical religious groups in Nicaragua argued that mediation should be encouraged to preserve the family.

The Nicaraguan government passed a law in 2012 to combat violence against women; it defined specific crimes, levels of punishment for aggressors and the steps the government should take to help women seek justice. But lawmakers recently voted to amend the law to allow state prosecutors to advise women to mediate with their abusers over certain types of violence, including "lesser injuries" that carry less than a five-year prison sentence.

Under Nicaragua's 2012 law on gender-related violence, femicide was defined as a specific crime against women, carrying a prison sentence of 25 to 30 years. But the system has been criticised as only about 12 per cent of cases get referred to court, according to a study by the Nicaraguan Center of Human Rights.

Amnesty International has criticised the government for the decision by lawmakers in Nicaragua to change the legislation on violence against women to offer victims mediation with their aggressors, arguing it could put women's lives in danger. "Instead of focusing on mediation and ways of letting abusers off the hook, the Nicaraguan authorities should look at ways of protecting women from violence and ensuring that those who abuse them face justice."

The Network of Women Against Violence promotes women's rights and campaigns against domestic violence with the help of NGOs; to educate women on domestic abuse, they have held workshops and helped with the formation of other women's groups to spread awareness. The Men Against Violence is a network with at least three groups in the country, working to change the attitudes and beliefs of the perpetrators.

Panama

The law criminalizes domestic abuse and family violence, for which it provides prison terms of two to four years. A new Code criminalises rape and spousal rape, with prison terms of five to 10 years, and eight to 10 years where there are aggravating circumstances. The new Code removes the provision that a perpetrator can marry a victim who is at least aged 14 and reduce the charge. It also mandates charging the perpetrator if the victim is between 14 and 18 years of age, unless there is proof of a long-standing relationship and the difference in age is less than five years. The majority of sexual crimes investigated by the PNP were cases of rape; however, statistics on prosecutions and convictions were not available. The PNP reported that it investigated every case relating to rape and domestic violence it received during the year.

MIDES' National Directorate of Women, the government agency responsible for promoting the rights of women, oversaw a national media campaign, "You Are Not Alone," which encouraged citizens to report incidents of domestic violence. MIDES also produced a directory of resources for female victims of domestic violence.

The government operated one shelter in Panama City for victims of domestic abuse and their children; the facility also occasionally sheltered trafficked victims. The shelter offered social, psychological, medical, and legal services. Between January and August, it provided accommodation and social services to approximately 54 women and 81 children. The law prohibits discrimination on the basis of gender, and women officially enjoyed the same rights as men, including rights under family law, property law, and the judicial penal system. Although the law recognizes joint or common property in marriages, the government did not allocate sufficient resources to enforce the law effectively. Although the law prohibits pregnancy discrimination, the International Labour Organization (ILO) Committee of Experts requested that the government take further measures to ensure that women on temporary contracts are not vulnerable to pregnancy discrimination.

The law mandates equal pay for men and women in equivalent jobs, but in practice women on average received wages that were 30 to 40 per cent lower than those received by men. MIDES, through the National Directorate of Women, promoted equality of women in the workplace and equal pay for equal work, they also work to reduce sexual harassment, and advocate legal reforms.

Paraguay

According to the Attorney General's Office, in 13 years there have been only four cases prosecuted where the wife continued with the case. In addition, the courts allow mediation of some family violence cases, although not provided for in the law. The

Secretariat of Women's Affairs' Office of Care and Orientation receives reports on violence against women and coordinates responses with the National Police, primary health care units, the Attorney-General's Office, and NGOs. Although these services were available only in Asunción, the secretariat partnered with several NGOs in other cities to assist in the protection of victims. The NGOs provided health and psychological assistance, including shelter to victims, and communicated with the authorities on behalf of the victims. The secretariat also conducted training courses for the police, health care workers, prosecutors, and others in assisting victims of trafficking and domestic violence.

The Women's November 25 Collective is an NGO operating a reception centre where female victims of violence received legal, psychological, and educational assistance. Another NGO, Kuna Aty, also offered services to abused women. There were no shelters for battered and abused women outside of Asunción. The country's first municipal shelter to care for victims of domestic violence, has the capacity to provide housing, medical, social, and psychological support to 30 victims and their children.

Peru
The law prohibits domestic violence, and penalties range from one month to six years in prison. The law gives judges and prosecutors the authority to prevent the convicted spouse or parent from returning to the family's home and authorizes the victim's relatives and unrelated persons living in the home to file complaints of domestic violence. It also allows health professionals to document injuries. The law requires police investigation of domestic violence to take place within five days and obliges authorities to extend protection to women and children who are victims of domestic violence.

The Ministry of Women and Social Development (MIMDES) centres reported 25,036 cases of domestic violence. The centres helped an average of 2,067 men and women per month. MIMDES also operated a toll-free hotline.

MIMDES and NGOs stated that many domestic abuse cases went unreported and that the majority of reported cases did not result in formal charges because of fear of retaliation or because of the expense of filing a complaint. The legal and physical protections offered were limited because of legal delays, ambiguities in the law, and the lack of shelters for victims. MIMDES ran the Women's Emergency Program, which sought to address the legal, psychological and medical problems facing victims. MIMDES operated 39 centres, bringing together police, prosecutors, counsellors, and public welfare agents together to help victims of domestic abuse.

Puerto Rico

Puerto Rico passed one of the most progressive domestic violence acts in Latin America and the Caribbean. It provided for protective orders for victims of Domestic Violence and criminalised physical and emotional violence, perpetrated by partners or ex partners. It also eliminated the right of a married man to non-consensual sex with his wife or partner.

The Domestic Abuse and Prevention Act of 1989 was amended in 2016 to "establish a body of measures addressed to prevent and fight domestic abuse in Puerto Rico: characterise the crimes of Abuse, Aggravated Abuse, Abuse Through Threat, Abuse Through Restriction of Liberty, and Conjugal Sexual Assault and fix penalties; empowers the Courts to make Orders for Protection for the victims of Domestic Abuse and expeditious procedure for the handling and adjudication of said orders; establish measures addressed to the prevention of domestic abuse. The law came under scrutiny when the Supreme Court upheld a lower court's reading that the victim of intimate domestic violence was not protected by Puerto Rico's domestic violence law because she was not married to the man who abused her. The woman who was separated but not yet divorced from her husband was battered by her new partner.[8]

The Puerto Rico Police Department (PRPD) has also come in for heavy criticism by the American Civil Liberties Union for failing to protect the victims of domestic violence. They reported that the PRPD has recorded "an appalling rise of complaints of domestic violence" perpetrated by PRPD officers, and that "nearly 1,500 complaints against police officers had been made from 2005 to 2010. At least 84 still-active officers have been arrested two or more times for domestic violence."[9]

St Kitts and Nevis

The Domestic Violence (Amended) Act No 10 of 2005 was enacted to provide better protection for victims of domestic violence. The Law criminalizes domestic violence and provides penalties of up to $5,000 fine and six months imprisonment for offenders. The Department of Gender Affairs said that many victims were hesitant to take action such as obtaining a restricting order against their abuser because of their financial dependence on the abuser. The Department reported that government established a safe house for the victims of abuse and began piloting gender sensitivity training for men. Counselling co-ordinated by the department was also available for survivors of abuse.[10]

St Lucia

The Domestic Violence (Summary Proceedings) Act was passed in St Lucia in 1995 and allows victims of domestic abuse to seek protection, occupation and/or tenancy orders from the court. In December 2004 the government announced that an amended Criminal Code would take effect from 1 January 2005. The new Code contains a number of provisions that addresses violence against women, including the introduction of "marital rape" as an offence as well as provisions that addresses stalking and workplace sexual harassment.

St Vincent and the Grenadines

The 1995 Domestic Violence (Summary Proceedings) Act is the legislation providing for protection orders, occupancy orders and tenancy orders. The Gender Affairs Division was created in 2001, with the objective of "prevention and eradication of domestic violence".

According to United States Country Report 2012 the law does not specifically criminalize domestic violence but charges can be brought against perpetrators under assault, battery or other similar laws.

Suriname

The government of Suriname in 2009 passed a law to combat domestic violence and activated the review of the Penal Code on Moral Offences, broadening opportunities for the prosecution of domestic violence perpetrators. The 2009 Law Combating Domestic Violence allowed for more severe punishment. The Bureau of Women and Child Policy under the Ministry of justice and Police conducted a domestic violence awareness and training campaign in 2009.

Trinidad and Tobago

The Domestic violence Act 27 of 1999 was amended in 2006 to "provide greater protection for victims of domestic violence." Its definition of domestic violence includes "physical, sexual, emotional or physiological or financial abuse committed by a person against a spouse, child or other person who is a member of the household or dependant". The Act provides for Protection orders and Enforcement orders, which can lead to imprisonment and/or fines for non-compliance. The court can also order counselling or therapy for the respondent – refusal to attend can lead to a fine.

The law gives Police Powers of Entry and Arrest. Police officers must respond "to a complaint or report alleging domestic violence weather or not the person making the complaint or the report is the victim." The police officer must complete a Domestic Violence Report Form to form part of the national Domestic Violence Register to be maintained by the Commissioner of Police.

Turks and Caicos Islands

The Domestic Violence Ordinance 2015 was enacted to "provide greater protection for victims and to make provision for the Issuing of Protection Orders", defining domestic violence to include:

• physical abuse and threats of physical abuse
• Sexual abuse or the threats of sexual abuse
• emotional, verbal or psychological abuse
• economic abuse

The Ordinance makes provision for protection orders, and a Magistrate has a range of measures to ensure protection and support for victims. The Magistrate may order the respondent, applicant or both to receive professional counselling or therapy from an agency or a programme that is approved by the department responsible for social services. The magistrate can make an order for the seizure of any firearm or offensive weapon in the possession of the respondent.

The ordinance outlines the Duty and Powers of Police Officers. Every complaint or report of domestic violence must be responded to by police officers regardless of who makes the complaint or report. The Police officer responding must complete a domestic violence report, which shall form part of the National Domestic Violence Register. Police can arrest a perpetrator at the scene of a domestic violence incident without a warrant of arrest and the police have a duty to provide assistance to the victim of domestic violence.

United States of America
The US federal probation and supervised release law requires first-time domestic violence offenders convicted of domestic violence crimes to attend court-approved non-profit offender rehabilitation programmes within a 50-mile radius of the individual's legal residence. Probation is mandatory for first-time domestic violence offenders not sentenced to a term of imprisonment.

The National Domestic Violence Hotline is a 24-hour, confidential, toll-free hotline created through the Family Violence prevention and Services Act. Hotline staff immediately connect the caller to a service provider in his or her area. Highly trained advocates provide support, information, referrals, safety planning, and crisis intervention in 170 languages to hundreds of thousands of domestic violence survivors.

Uruguay
In the kind of exemplary action needed by leaders in the region, Uruguayan President Jose Mujica made a surprise appearance on the streets of Montevideo, distributing flyers to pedestrians in a bid to stop domestic violence. "Men, learn to lose. Never use violence against women," said the flyers, which Mujica handed out to a group of teenagers on a street in the heart of

the Uruguayan capital. The teenagers then invited Mujica to a nearby public school for a discussion, according to a government website in November 2011, where he told them: "Don't allow yourself to be mistreated." He also reminded the male students never to hit a woman under any circumstances. "The young boys have to start thinking before they leave home," he said.

Uruguay reported to the UN that its application of the Convention on the Elimination of All Forms of Discrimination Against Women (CEDAW) has led to the development of several actions including:

1. Creation of four specialized courts in the Department of Montevideo.
2. Night courts throughout the country to deal with emergency situations.
3. Creation of the National Advisory Council against Domestic Violence.
4. Establishment of departmental commissions for combating domestic violence.
5. Training for operators of the public system, with an emphasis on the judicial, police and health systems, headed by the National Women's Institute through the project for "strengthening justice institutions in relation to gender for equitable development."
6. The National Programme for Women's Health and Gender (PNSMG) of the Ministry of Public Health (MSP) is coordinating efforts to have health authorities, institutions and personnel address domestic violence as a public health problem.

Domestic violence officially became a crime when it became part of the penal code in 1995. The following year, Uruguay ratified the Inter-American Convention on the Prevention, Punishment and Eradication of Violence against Women. The Convention of Belém do Pará, as it became known, adopted the definition of gender-based violence provided in the 1993 United Nations Declaration on the Elimination of Violence Against Women, and included "physical, sexual or psychological violence that occurs within the family or domestic unit or within any other interpersonal relationship."

In 2002, Uruguay passed legislation that addressed the issue of domestic violence with Law No. 17514, which provides measures for the prevention, early detection, treatment and eradication of domestic violence. However, there has been some criticism that the law is unclear about domestic violence and sexual crimes in marriage and that prevention and interdisciplinary diagnostic teams were not actually put in place in most cases of domestic violence. In those cases where the aggressor is punished, victims are rarely notified in advance of the aggressor's release from custody, as the law requires. There is almost no state money dedicated to domestic violence, which means that the majority of training for judges, police officials, health and social workers, and the like, comes from the non-profit sector, which is unable to perform this work on the broad scale needed for true eradication of domestic violence.

Critics argue that while laws and policies are in place to address gender inequality, domestic violence, and femicide, poor implementation has meant little real change for women. Of the few victims bringing charges against their abusers, many feel let down by the system. Court-ordered measures to protect victims are issued in only approximately 6 per cent of cases. Moreover, most perpetrators who violate the court-ordered measures are rarely punished they say.

US Virgin Islands

Domestic violence is a criminal act as defined by Title 16 Virgin Islands Code Section 91, which provides for protection from battering, assault, burglary, threats and attempts at threats against a person who may be protected under the law, including: a spouse, a former spouse, parent or child, person related by blood or marriage, household member, a person in an intimate relationship with the perpetrator.

Protection orders can be obtained from the Families Division of the Supreme Court. A temporary or permanent restricting order may obtained for a period of 24 hours or more, depending. Domestic violence advocates from private agencies or from the Virgin Islands Police Department may help with filing a Restraining Order.

Domestic violence victims are treated as government witnesses and cannot "drop" charges. That decision lies with the Attorney General or an Assistant Attorney General.

Venezuela

Amnesty International called Venezuela's 2007 Law on the Right of Women to a Life Free of Violence "an example for the rest of the region," but said practical implementation of the law has been slow.

The Fundamental Law on the Right of Women to Live Free of Violence (LODMVLV) proscribes 19 forms of violence against women, including psychological violence, harassment, threats, physical violence, domestic violence, sexual violence, forced sexual penetration, forced prostitution, sexual slavery, sexual harassment, work-related violence, property-related and economic violence, obstetric violence, forced sterilization, media violence, institutional violence, symbolic violence, trafficking in women, girls and adolescents, and trading in women, girls and adolescents (Venezuela 2007, Art. 15).

The LODMVLV also lists 13 measures for protection and security, which include providing temporary shelter, removing the perpetrator from the home if safety is at risk, requesting a judge to restrict the perpetrator's visits to the victim, imposing restrictions on how close a perpetrator may get to the victim, requesting temporary arrest, posting police at the victim's residence, confiscating the perpetrator's weapons, obliging the perpetrator to provide the victim with financial resources for subsistence if a relationship of economic dependency exists.

In cases of necessity or urgency, the receiving agency may directly ask the court that handles cases of violence against women, with functions of oversight, hearing and measures, to issue an arrest order. The resolution ordering the arrest must always be justified. The court must decide within 24 hours of the request. The punishments listed for the 19 forms of violence against women vary depending on the crime, but include fines and imprisonment. President Maduro signed into law in 2015 the reform of the Fundamental Law on the Right of Women to Live Free From Violence, which was originally passed in 2007.

The Reform includes femicide as an act of hate towards women as a felony, punishable by 25 to 30 years' imprisonment in the Federal prison.

It has been clear to some of us working with the perpetrators of domestic violence, that laws alone will not stop domestic violence; tackling the root causes of the violence is what will make the difference. From the actions undertaken by governments to end violence to women, it is clear that most of the resources are directed at supporting the survivors. Some countries provide support for perpetrators, though there are not enough projects in the region to make a significant difference to the overall violence – but it is a start that has to be built on, if we are to see an end to violence in the region.

Notes to Chapter 8

1   BBC News, 27 July 2016.
2   Anastasia Maloney, "2008-2016 Safe World for Women. Colombia: Domestic Violence is women's worst enemy". TrustLaw, April 2012.
3   Centre for Gender and Refugee Studies (CGRS), 14 August 2015, p. 5.
4   CGRS, 14 August 2015, p. 7.
5   CGRS, 14 August 2015, p. 7
6   Immigration and Refugee Board of Canada: "France: Availability of state protection and support services in Guadeloupe for women victims of domestic violence" (2012-April 2016) [Fra105500. FE], 14 June 2016.
7   Honduras – Committee against Torture – Violence against Women – July 2016.
8   Marianne Mollmann, "A Step Backward for Puerto Rican Women", *Puerto Rican Daily Sun,* 4 August 2011.
9   American Civil Liberties Union website 2017.
10 United States Department of State, Country Reports for 2016.

Chapter 9

GOVERNMENT'S RESPONSIBILITY TO END VIOLENCE

Domestic violence is endemic in most countries but in the Americas has reached pandemic proportions, with recent research showing Latin America as the worst place in the world to be a woman. The region has a huge problem with "machismo" and domestic violence thrives in a macho world. Governments can no longer ignore the problem and urgent solutions are needed if we are to end the explosion in violence. Our history of violence is largely responsible for the culture of machismo that prevails, but we can and must do more to challenge this culture of violence. There can be no ending of domestic violence without ending all violence.

We in the Americas are no longer in immediate danger of being wiped out by our neighbours, but the socialization for violence continues unabated. The changed political and social conditions give us opportunity to end the socialization for violence. Governments can do much to speed up the process of change – and speed is needed, since the longer the conditions that nurture machismo thrive, the bigger the problem of violence for future generations.

Only governments have the resources and power to end the violence and it is a dereliction of duty to pass the buck to charitable organisations, women's organizations or non-governmental organisations (NGOs) to solve the problem. Our governments must provide leadership in finding solutions to ending the violence. It is not enough to pass a few well-meaning laws and not provide the resources and necessary action to end this blight on the development of our societies. Violence is a huge drain on our financial resources and governments need to invest in finding solutions to ending it.

The measures taken by most Western governments have largely been ineffective, as they present no clear, consistent theory on the causes of domestic violence, much less on the solutions to ending it. It is no accident that neo-liberal governments are not prepared to address the root causes of domestic violence, as the solutions would undermine the very basis of their existence. There is no point in adopting a failed neo-liberal approach to ending domestic violence in the Americas. Identifying the root causes of domestic violence and doing something about them is what will end it – not longer prison sentences and building more refuges. This is not a strategy to end domestic violence, at the very best these actions may contain it.

The United Nations made it clear that tackling domestic violence is the responsibility of governments and have outlined 43 measures that governments need implement, to reduce violence in society. Most governments in the region have responded to some of the recommendations and have passed laws making domestic violence a crime. Although the measures may not go far enough, they are a good starting point to effect change; it is worth reminding governments of some of these:

1. Legal and policy framework, including adherence to the Convention on the Elimination of All Forms of Discrimination Against Women (CEDAW) and other relevant international treaties; equality for men and women in the constitution; national action plans on combating violence against women; the allocation of an adequate budget; legislation covering all forms of Violence Against Women.
2. Criminal justice system, including investigation (with respect for victims), prosecution and punishment of perpetrators.
3. Remedies for victims of violence against women, including access to justice, reparation for harm suffered, guarantees of non-repetition and prevention (protection / restraining orders).
4. Support services, including access to shelters, medical, psychological, legal aid and other support.
5. Modify attitudes and behaviour regarding social and cultural patterns of conduct of women and men by eliminating stereotypes that legitimize, exacerbate or tolerate violence

against women. Include national campaigns on zero tolerance against violence to women.

6. Capacity building and training of all those who respond to violence against women, such as law enforcement officers, immigration, judicial and medical personnel and social workers.

7. Data and statistics, including promoting research, collecting data and compiling statistics.

However, despite these recommendations and numerous declarations against violence to women and the billions of dollars spent by the UN; by their own admission, little has changed for women in 40 years. This is partly because the recommended measures do not address the root causes of domestic violence. Another approach from simply removing the woman from the domestic situation and imprisoning the perpetrator must be imagined. Going after the root causes of domestic violence will mean implementing strategies that only radical progressive governments would dare contemplate.

The region is facing a pandemic in violence and we need learn from examples of how governments successfully respond to end pandemic. A recent example of successful government action defeating a pandemic is that of Sri Lanka. The World Health Organization (WHO) has certified Sri Lanka as a malaria-free nation, in what it called a "truly remarkable achievement". Sri Lanka had been one of the most malaria-affected countries in the mid-20th century. But the WHO said the country had begun an anti-malaria campaign that successfully targeted the mosquito borne parasite that caused the disease, not just the mosquitoes. Health education and effective surveillance also helped the campaign. The WHO statement said: "The change in strategy was unorthodox but highly effective. Mobile malaria clinics in high transmission areas meant that prompt and effective treatment could reduce the parasite reservoir and the possibility of further transmission." There had been no new cases for three years and to prevent the parasite from re-entering the country they were working with local and international partners to maintain surveillance and screening, it said.[1]

I would not want to insult the feelings of any of my fellow men by comparing them with mosquitoes, but the example of this case is just too good to let go. Domestic violence has often been compared to a disease; in the case of Latin America it is best described as a pandemic and "unorthodox methods" will have to be used to defeat it. There are lessons to be learned from the way Sri Lanka eradicated malaria:

1. They Identified the Problem. The mosquito, they deduced was responsible for spreading the illness. Men have been identified as the main perpetrators of violence, yet the focus of most government action on tackling domestic violence has been to focus on the mainly women survivors. To solve the problem of domestic violence more resources need to be directed at the solution: changing attitude and behaviour of the mainly men who perpetrate violence. The survivors still have to be kept safe and need resources. But it is doubtful that Sri Lanka could have defeated malaria had they directed the vast majority of their energies and resources on only treating the victims of malaria.

2. Diagnosed the Problem. The scientists correctly diagnosed it was a virus that was causing malaria and that was carried by the mosquito. In the case of domestic violence, the west has correctly diagnosed men as the problem. We can equate the malaria virus with an imaginary violence virus carried mainly, but not exclusively, by men. In the case of malaria, the scientists targeted the virus to understand how it works and rendered it harmless. We need do the same with perpetrators if we are to defeat domestic violence – we must understand why it is men who mainly use violence. Scientists have identified a gene responsible for violence, but humans are more complex than viruses and there are divided opinions among scientists about the workings of the gene. Some have argued that the gene is responsible for men's violence and that men cannot help but be violent. However, a sizeable and respected body of scientists argue that although genes have a role, it is a very small and insignificant one, compared to the role of

socialization: that the violence is mainly learned behaviour. If we choose to accept the arguments of the "can't help themselves" advocates, we throw them in jail and throw away the key; if not, we look for solutions to interrupting the learned, violent behaviour. This is the challenge our governments must face up to.

3. They targeted the parasite that caused malaria. The Sri Lanka government targeted the mosquito and provided the resources needed over a protracted time, to solve the problem. There are no quick fix solutions to ending domestic violence and no amount of slogans and walks in the park will solve it. The parasite, to be targeted in the case of domestic violence, is patriarchy. The popular sound bite answer in the west, as to the cause of domestic violence is usually "power and control", with countless "wheels" describing this; but they hardly speak to the real root cause of domestic violence -patriarchy. Although there is some value in the "power and control" response, these are learned behaviours that can be unlearned.

4. They provided mobile clinics in high transmission areas for prompt and effective treatment. Imagine what this would mean for domestic violence – having highly trained units moving to an area with high incidence of domestic violence, to resolve the problems. With the unit taking the perpetrator into custody and providing counselling, and with support and possible refuge for the survivor. With specialist support for any children affected by the violence. Every major city and problem area in the region could benefit enormously from such support and governments must think seriously about providing them.

5. The Sri Lankans prevented contagion, working with local and international partners.

Domestic violence deserves the approach used to defeat malaria in Sri Lanka. Our governments need to declare a pandemic and take the drastic measures needed to end violence on the whole or the future will indeed be bleak for the region. Violence affects every aspect of our lives, but it is the majority of poor who bear the brunt of its consequences, or we would soon see a serious attempt to ending it. Violence affects the entire region and the measures needed to end the violence are the same for all of our communities. Tackling the problem of violence as a regional one will help stop the forced migration of people seeking safety and security in neighbouring countries. There are no "one size fits all" solutions to ending domestic violence; but our shared history means that we have a lot in common and the solutions will be the same for the region. Understanding our history will help in providing answers to end the violence.

A core responsibility of government is the protection of its citizens and especially its most vulnerable citizens. The General Assembly of the United Nations adopted and proclaimed the Universal Declaration of Human Rights (UDHR) on 10 December 1948 in Paris. The Declaration's foremost statement – "All human beings are born with equal and inalienable rights and fundamental freedoms" – is the first international recognition that all human beings have fundamental rights and freedoms; the sentiments expressed are just as relevant today as when the declaration was first made, and most of our governments have signed up to them, with one notable exception: the USA. Everyone in our region deserves to have their human rights respected, regardless of colour, creed, age or gender and we need hold our governments accountable if they fail to protect us.

The problem we face is that most modern states are rooted in patriarchal rule, which legitimises inequality and exploitation, especially by gender, class, age and race. Only governments that champion the rights of people to enjoy a life free from oppression can end the violence. There can be no real change to the violence experienced in the Americas if governments do not put people before profits. Only when the state truly respects women and takes action to defend their human rights can the situation for women radically improve. Too often, in the recent past, governments in the region have not protected but destroyed its citizens.

Inequality, which has been acknowledged as one of the root causes of violence, even by the World Bank, will only end when there is a will by governments to do so. We need look no further than Honduras, as an example of how a government fails to protect its citizens. With its "deepening of the neoliberal programme and the intensified re-militarization of the country. In 2011 the government passed a Law for the Promotion and Protection of Investment, which provided legal certainties and guarantees for large investors that they will not face tax increases and lawsuits ... under the Law foreign companies can open a subsidiary in four days, and mega projects valued at $50 million or more will be able to access a speed-up permitting process, allowing them to gain all of their state and local permits within thirty days. [President Pepe] Lobo's government also passed laws decimating labour rights and allowing foreign companies to purchase nationally owned land and resources."[2]

Inequality is what fuels the violence. Despite no regional wars, except the war on drugs:

Latin America and the Caribbean (LAC) has been declared the most dangerous region in the world, with 23.9 per cent homicides per 100,000 inhabitants in 2012 compared to 9.7, 4.4, 2.7, and 2.9 for Africa, North America, Asia and Europe respectively. LAC accounts for only eight per cent of the world's population but for 37 per cent of the world's homicides. Eight out of the 10 most violent countries in the world are in LAC. In 2013, of the top 50 most violent countries of the world, 42 were in the region, including the top 16. The annual growth rate of homicides (3.7 per cent) dramatically outstripped population growth (1.5 per cent) from 2005 to 2012. In 2012 alone 145,759 people in LAC fell victim to homicide corresponding to 400.44 homicides committed per day and 4.17 homicides every 15 minutes.[3]

According to a recent World Bank study covering the past two decades, nearly every region in the world has grown safer, or at least stayed the same, except Latin America. Even recent and ongoing wars in the Middle East cannot compete with us, with Brazil alone recording more deaths by homicide in 2015 than the combined loss of life in Syria, Afghanistan and Iraq. Radical action is needed if we are to reverse this trend, and needed urgently.

Facing social problems is nothing new in the Americas. After a spate of labour unrest in the British West Indies in the 1940s, the British responded by setting up an enquiry into the disturbances. The result was the 1945 Report of West India Royal Commission known as The Moyne Report, which, as Gordon Lewis points out, "had talked, boldly, of constructive efforts to provide a satisfactory alternative to the original cultures now lost to the West Indian peoples. But in practice that grand concept declined into the game of administrative reorganization so beloved of the colonial service mentality."[4] In 1946 Professor Thomas Simey published *Welfare and Planning in the West Indies*, a work that critiqued colonial mismanagement and attitudes up to and including the findings and recommendations of Lord Moyne. Simey concluded: "It is impossible to deal with the social problems of the West Indies … without first inventing new tools to facilitate the task, or in other words, without first promoting advances in the applied sciences of social engineering."[5] No action was taken, since the prevailing neoliberal thinking in Britain at the time was very much against the state intervening to fix social problems. We can afford no such liberal sentiments in the region today and must take decisive action to end the violence engulfing us.

Research has long established that "violence breeds violence". If we do not accept this truism, we are in for a difficult time, as the violence being perpetrated in the region can only lead to more violent acts. In almost every country in the region there is an upward trend in violence – massively so in a few countries. Our governments have to face the reality of our situation and take decisive action to stem the tide of violence now, or we will have failed future generations.

Too much is at stake to leave defeating violence only to women's organizations, charitable organizations and non-governmental organizations (NGOs). The scale of the problem is too great for them to make the kind of difference, in the time required, to put an end to the violence stalking our region. The 1938 Moyne Commission by the British recognised that the problems of the Caribbean were so deep, it would take social engineering to fix them. Today, violence is even more serious in

---

the region. These are some key measures regional governments must consider in an effort to combat the violence:

Ministry of Violence Prevention

A minister for violence prevention with enough staff and resources as is necessary to be effective to stop the violence – a ministry staffed with criminologists and experts in culture change, with joined-up thinking and strategy, working with people and organizations committed to ending violence. This ministry will have to be adequately resourced to be effective. It will be worth every penny spent in the long run, as violence is wreaking havoc on our economies. The financial burden of building prisons and added cost of imprisonment, the cost of victim support, the police officers, the social workers, the courts, the hospitals, the time lost from work, the needless loss of life, the psychological damage and repair costs run into billions. The emotional price caused by domestic violence cannot be quantified.

The home and school are key battlegrounds and parents and teachers must be supported with information and skills to combat violence. In some cases unpopular draconian action may be necessary to bring an end to the pandemic. Violent patterns of behaviour are deeply ingrained in our region and it will take a consorted, strategic, informed, scientific approach to stop the passing on of these patterns to the next generation.

It is encouraging to see the growing co-operation between Latin American and Caribbean (LAC) governments to solve their common problems. At the inaugural meeting of 26 May 2017, government delegates signed the document accepting responsibility for Sustainable Development. According to ECLAC, the document that was adopted by the United Nations General Assembly in 2015 established 17 Sustainable Development Goals (SDGs) and 169 targets for the year 2030. The Foreign Affairs Secretary of Mexico, Luis Videgaray who hosted the meeting, said the forum's first meeting left behind two important messages "Multilateralism works and is important," he added: "It has become clear that Latin America and the Caribbean presents itself before the world as a region that expresses its leadership proudly, where precedents are set and we dare to innovate." Alicia Barcena,

ECLAC's Executive Secretary, was ecstatic about the forum's first session, attended by some 789 participants: 208 delegates from 35 countries (31 Latin American and the Caribbean and four observers from other regions); 285 representatives from 198 civil society organizations; 157 delegates from 39 inter-governmental bodies; 125 special guests and representatives from the private sector and academia and 11 parliamentarians from eight countries. In their proclamation the regional governments stressed that the attainment of gender equality and empowerment of women and girls will contribute in a crucial way to achieving the SDGs.[6]

We must dare to dream that we can stop the tide of violence engulfing us, but it is only action that will change the situation. Some will find the measures needed unpalatable, others may think them impossible, but we cannot afford to do nothing. These are some of the actions that governments must consider in the battle to end the violence:

End inequality

Recognised as one of the main underlying causes of violence in society, reducing inequality must be a priority for any government hoping to reduce domestic violence. To pay women less for doing the same work as men reinforces the belief that men are superior; equal pay and opportunity for women is a central plank of ending domestic violence.

Ending inequality generally is desirable and governments must take measures to reverse the situation in which most workers find themselves. The Center for Economic and Policy Research in 2013 cited Honduras as the most unequal country in Latin America, with 10 per cent of highest earners controlling 42 per cent of national income and the lowest 10 per cent of earners only receiving 0.17 per cent of income nationally. It is no coincidence that Honduras holds the record for the highest levels of violence in the world. Researchers found that "in areas where wealth and extreme poverty cohabit, violence tends to occur more frequently."[7]

Inequality is not the only problem as demography also plays an important role in the incidence of violence. Historically, most lawbreakers the world over have been young men; the prison populations everywhere are proof of this. Demographers routinely use a shorthand expression to describe this group – the "barbarians".

Nations with the most violence tend to be those with the largest number of "barbarians", with most violent crime usually "barbarian" on "barbarian." In Brazil young men aged between 15 and 19 suffer nearly double the national homicide rate. In Mexico, according to the World Health Organization and the Pan American Health Organization, the male homicide rate in 2002 was 29.6 per 100,000 while the female homicide rate was 3.1, a ratio of almost 10 to one.

According to a World Bank report *Ninis in Latin America*, one in five youths aged between 15 and 24 in the region neither work nor study. The absolute numbers of "ninis" grew by 2 million to nearly 20 million during the past decade, despite the region's booming economies in the early 2000s. The "ninis" amount to about 20 per cent of the region's total number of youths. This is nearly twice the 11 per cent who neither work nor study in the industrialised countries. Honduras and El Salvador have the highest percentage of "ninis" about 25 per cent of their young populations (again these two with the highest murder rates), while Peru's percentage of "ninis" is 11 per cent of its young (with a lower murder rate). In absolute numbers Brazil, Columbia and Mexico have the largest numbers of "ninis". Throughout Latin America, about two-thirds of all youths who neither work nor study are girls, many of whom abandon school because of pregnancies. But the fastest rising group within the "nini" population is that of young men, many of whom end up recruited by gangs or organized crime.[8] Government action to end the unemployment of youth will make a difference in violence levels.

Defeat machismo

The mostly men in government in the region must take a stand against macho culture that is fuelling the violence. Most women's groups in the region say machismo is a main cause of violence to women. Ending domestic violence means defeating machismo; this will not be easy or quick, but failure to do so will consign us to a yet more violent future. Changing the culture of violence requires government action, with the support and input of all parents and care givers. Interrupting the socialisation for violence and sexist conditioning are crucial tools in the struggle against domestic violence. Governments can take action to end the celebration of machismo in advertising and television. This is vital in combating the violent stereotyping of men.

Provide justice

Lack of Justice is a key contributing factor to high levels of violence in the region. The fact that many criminals simply walk away from their crimes, has led to widespread lack of faith in the fairness and honesty of law enforcement and the criminal justice system. A recent public opinion survey by the leading Latin American polling firm, Latinobarómetro, revealed that more than half of Latin Americans had "little or no" confidence in the police, and just one in five thought that poor people had equal access to the justice system.

Mexico is a prime example: criminals operate here with near total wild abandon, as only about one in four crimes are ever reported to the police. Some argue – perhaps because people have lost trust in the police, or experience has taught them – that contacting the police is a waste of time. Only about three per cent of lawbreakers ever come to trial in Mexico and few of these are ever convicted. Hardly anyone is ever jailed for committing a crime and if a violent criminal is convicted and actually sent to prison, it is relatively easy to escape, as evidenced by the notorious televised case of drug lord Joaquin Guzman, who disappeared before our very eyes down a mile-long tunnel to freedom. Twice escaped, he was recaptured and only in January 2017 was extradited to the USA to face murder, weapons and drug-trafficking charges. His case is reminiscent of the notorious Colombian drug baron Pablo Escobar, killed in 1993, who was allowed to design his own prison cell, in a deal struck with the authorities.

Outlaw the hitting of children

Protecting children from violence is a key element of the work to defeat violence and governments must pass laws to protect children from all forms of violence. Parents have to be supported with parenting skills to end the abuse of children and governments must provide support for parents. This is probably the single most important measure to end violence in society. The Scandinavian countries have done this and are now seeing the benefits of less violence and crime in their communities – not anarchy and lawlessness, as some of the "spare the rod" brigade would have us believe would be the end result, but peace and prosperity. Governments in the region have to be bold here and they have the support of the UN in outlawing the mistreatment of children. A good place to start is to outlaw corporal punishment in schools. Dr Rupert Roopnarine the Minister of Education has shown the way in Guyana by doing exactly that. But there are still too many ready to argue how much a "good beating" has done for them, while our communities slip further into the abyss of yet more violence.

Education for all
Research has shown that education makes a difference in the perpetration of violence. Governments must ensure that all children have opportunity for education. Too many of our children leave school with little education. Measures must be in place to support students to further education or we will have higher and higher levels of crime and violence. Better to spend on education rather than prisons.

Enforce domestic violence law
It is not enough to produce domestic violence legislation and not provide the resources to back it up. Perpetrators must get a clear message that domestic violence will not be tolerated and that every incident will be pursued until justice is delivered. For far too long men have got away with domestic violence and many believe they can continue to do so. This perception must be changed. When the justice system fails survivors of abuse, it sends the wrong message and encourages the abuser, who often goes on to even worse excesses. Nothing erodes confidence in government like a lack of justice and work must be done to ensure a robust

system of accountability in the justice system, at every level. A study concluded that the number-one cause of rising violence in Mexico was the defective judicial system.[9] The police are often on the frontline of domestic violence; it is important that they are fit for purpose. Research has shown that the incidence of domestic violence is often higher in the police force than the population at large. Recent research found that nine out of 10 domestic violence allegations made against Chicago police officers by their spouses and children led to no disciplinary action. The force responds to 500 domestic violence cases a day but the team found that since 2000 there had been 5,280 domestic violence complaints filed against the Chicago police. According to request for information report 92 per cent of the complaints led to no disciplinary action.[10]

Control violent TV programming
There is an abundance of research to show that watching violence is highly addictive and children often become desensitised by the violence, making them less likely to protest it and often perpetrate it. Children are often exposed to more violence than adults and will often see more violent images than their parents. We must have controls on what the young are exposed to and a sensible threshold for violent movies or programmes must be implemented to protect young minds. Parents need to be aware of the dangers of children watching violence.

Support for children who witness domestic violence
Much of domestic violence happens in the home but all too often children witness it in public places and on the streets. Most of the perpetrators I have counselled have been exposed to domestic violence -seen it or heard it through the walls. Boys who witness domestic violence must get help as those who witness domestic violence are twice as likely to abuse their own partners and children when they become adults.[11] Other researchers have confirmed that "Children who witness violence at home display emotional and behavioural disturbances as diverse as withdrawal, low self-esteem, nightmares, self-blame and aggression against peers, family members and property".[12] There is need for projects providing support for children who witness domestic violence if we are to stem the tide of violence.

Protect young people from violent video games

The proliferation of violent video games makes matters worse, and parents need be aware of the damage violent video games do to children, too many of whom have access to extremely violent video games. The American Academy of Paediatrics has recommended that "all children under the age of six should be shielded from-on screen violence due to their inability to distinguish fantasy from reality. They also insisted that in video games, humans or living targets should never be shot for points."[13] Nevertheless, these games often end up in very young hands since parents are unaware of the damage they do. Some of these same videos are used to prepare army recruits for combat situation as they go into battle and are quite extreme.

Ban boxing on television

Boxing is a highly rewarded and regarded sport popular in all of the Americas, with some like Manny Pacquiao and the late Muhammad Ali greatly revered. This is the only sport whose object is to cause pain and unconsciousness, and should be banned from television. Restricting boxing on television will not be popular, but this so-called sport is responsible for much of the violent stereotyping of men and increasingly of women in the Americas, and government must take action. Research has shown that more men die in the streets next day after a much publicised boxing match. Many boxers die in the ring and most suffer some kind of brain damage; also many fighters have been arrested as perpetrators of domestic violence. We cannot stop adults wanting to bash themselves, but it does not have to be on television. At the very least, this so-called sport should be sidelined to paying channels.

Support for perpetrator programmes

Work with perpetrators is still relatively new and needs time and support to develop. There can be no ending of domestic violence unless men take responsibility for their violence. Governments must provide resources to support men's groups that counsel perpetrators to end their violence, or the problems will only persist. There is some evidence that programmes which work with men individually before they join a group produce best results.

Support progressive art and culture

Promote and support the arts. Every opportunity to raise awareness and educate people about domestic violence should be utilised. Artists who promote non-violence in song and in writings should be encouraged and recognised for their efforts on the stage.

Strict gun and knife control laws

Much of the problem with gun crime in the region originates in the USA, with its Second Amendment. One can understand the anxiety of the founding fathers in 1791, wanting to protect their infant revolution, thinking that "A well-regulated militia being necessary to the security of a free state, the right of the people to keep and bear arms shall not be infringed." Well, that might have been acceptable 200 years ago but the USA has to wake up. We are in the 21st century and no country would dream of invading a nation with the world's largest arsenal of weapons, including nuclear weapons capable of wiping out the entire world several times over.

The Republic can no longer afford to be held hostage to the gun lobby, as they put profits before people. There is no need for the population to be armed to the teeth – the state, whose responsibility it is to protect, already is. Too many lives, in all of the Americas, pay the cost. The National Rifle Association with their blind greed, regardless of the pain caused, must be checked by legislation. When a two-year-old can shoot and kill siblings or parents, it is time to pay attention. When disgruntled teenagers can shoot up their schools on a regular basis, it is time to end the ease with which guns can be purchased. When thousands of women die each year because of guns used in domestic violence, it is time to call a halt. When black and Latino communities are at war with themselves, it is time to revoke the right to bear arms.

Most of the murders in the region are committed with the use of hand guns and the easy availability of firearms is a prime factor in the rising tide of violence in the Americas. Most of the weapons used originate in the United States, which is by far the largest manufacturer of weapons in the world and also the most active in the international trade in firearms. The second amendment is literally killing us and governments in the region must take responsibility for the amount of guns in its citizen's hands.

Pew Research Centre in 2014 found that 52 per cent of US citizens say it is right to own guns, and the first five months of 2015 saw 17,083 gun incidents resulting in 4,454 deaths. The countries in closest proximity to the USA find it easier to acquire guns and have similar high rates of gun violence. The tracing of weapons used in crimes reveals that 8 of 10 crime guns used in Jamaica were bought in Florida. In Mexico it was found that 9 of 10 guns used there were purchased in US border states, especially from Texas, New Mexico and Arizona.

End war on drugs

The so-called "war on drugs" is costing us dearly and is responsible for much violence affecting many countries in the region. This is a phony war declared by the USA. They choose to fight their battle with drug addiction in the rest of the Americas. It is our young people who mostly die. It is us who have our rural populations traumatised and often displaced and live with the consequences of this "war on drugs".

While the drug war's stated goals are drug eradication and reduction of trafficking from Latin America into the United States, its failures have raised questions about potential ulterior motives. Dawn Paley in *Drug War Capitalism* argues that there are economic motives for militarising this resource rich region. "We should use a new metric to understand the success of Plan Colombia, one that examines how it benefits transnational capital," Paley told teleSUR English. "If we were to examine the results of Plan Colombia based on how it deepened neoliberalism in Colombia, we would have to recognize that it was a success."

The Global Commission on Drug Policy in its report, Taking Control: Pathways to Drug Policies That Work, released by former heads of state and other global political figures, called the drug war a failure and called for the decriminalization of drugs, including heroin and cocaine. It also criticised the militarization of the war on drugs, which "...led to infiltration and corruption of governments, armies and police by cartels, and a culture of impunity for human rights abuses, especially extra-judicial killings and disappearances."

There is nothing new in using legislation to end drug war; the US Congress in 1933 repealed the 18th amendment to the US constitution, in order to end the period of gang and related violence, brought on by Prohibition – which banned the manufacture, transportation and sale of intoxicating liquors – resulting in the lucrative, illegal trade in alcohol.

Despite the scandals, murders, disappearances and human rights abuses that plagued the US-sponsored Plan Colombia; this drug war model was exported north to Mexico under the name of the Merida Initiative in 2008. This "Plan Mexico," along with former Mexican president Felipe Calderon's use of the country's military to fight the so-called drug war, has brought similar results. Molly Molloy, a border and Latin American researcher at New Mexico State University Library, argues that the number of people murdered in the country since 2007 is much higher than Mexican government claims. Using statistics from various Mexican government agencies, she estimates the number of dead to be at least 155,000, in contrast to the 80,000 to 100,000 often cited in media reports. She added, that her figures don't take into account the tens of thousands of Mexicans who have been forcibly disappeared.

"The Merida Initiative money provided to Mexico and Plan Colombia funding mostly goes to fund fighting drug organizations with violence," said Molloy. "My observation is that this generates more and more violence and does nothing to destroy drug organizations."

In 2012, according to the research and analysis website InSight Crime, makeshift ovens and charred bodies were found in the Mexican state of Michoacán, illustrating how Colombian paramilitary-government tactics travelled north. Amnesty International also published a report that stated cases of torture and human rights abuses by Mexico's police and armed forces increased 600 per cent between 2010 and 2013. Despite this militarized approach with its history of increased violence, the presidents of Guatemala and Honduras have called for a Central American version of Plan Colombia to be funded by the United States.

Paley contends that "the drug war serves as a tool for expanding capitalism...the drug war serves to reconfigure trafficking routes and, as it does so, brings further militarization and violence to said regions."[14] It is the poor who suffer most, as imperialism yet again forces indigenous people off their mineral-rich lands in the region. "I am a survivor, I lost my whole family. They killed my father, my mother, an older brother, two sisters, and a younger brother. When they killed my mother she was pregnant," Osorio Chenh. "The army destroyed our community. They wanted to eliminate the whole community, but still, thank God, we survived. I don't know how, how we could survive all of that, but thanks be to God that here we are alive."[15] The dangers of drug war loom large in Guyana with its wide-open, porous borders. There has been a phenomenal increase in the number of drug mules arrested, as dealers attempt to get their drugs to the USA in all manner of ways, including in fruits, food, drinks, timber, coal, carvings, false compartment suitcases, and their bodies – this coupled with discovery of abandoned fast boats, an airplane, even a submarine under construction, in the vast, sparsely populated interior of Guyana.

Experts say the spike in violence against women is worst in areas hit hard by the drugs war; this is not surprising, for there are similarities to what happens in countries at war. Women are often the victims of rape in countries fighting war; in the drug wars, women in conflict zones are often seen as "territory" to be conquered, and raping and murdering women a way to intimidate rival gangs and the local population. Reports indicate that victims are getting younger and the attacks more violent. In north-eastern Mexico, a major drugs battleground, the number of women slain jumped over 500 per cent between 2001 and 2010, according to a study by Mexico's National Commission to Prevent and Eradicate Violence against Women.

Corruption and incompetence are rampant in under-funded police forces across Mexico and the vast majority of murders are never solved. Families routinely complain that police show scant interest in the cases of missing women.

The countries that experienced some of the most brutal wars – Guatemala, El Salvador, Nicaragua and Honduras – are now the ones with the highest levels of violence. Under the dictatorships women were routinely raped and disappeared; now they are routinely raped, disfigured and dumped with the rubbish. Generations of men dehumanised by warfare, with little education and job prospects, have produced men with little or no feelings of empathy.

Conclusion:

Nicaragua was attacked by Amnesty International for attempting to try something different from what the West has done – with failure so far. They were criticised for legislating to make it possible to try mediation in domestic violence cases. This was immediately seized on as potentially making it more dangerous for women. If that same approach was adopted with violent conflicts the world over, we would never have peace. The majority of survivors have consistently said that what they want is for the violence to end – not necessarily the relationship. As one who has successfully worked with perpetrators, I have at times counselled couples – not necessarily trying to save the relationship. Having an amicable parting, especially when children are involved, is at times very important for all concerned. I would only caution that individual work with the perpetrator must be done before any attempts at relationship counselling, which should only be attempted if the survivor welcomes it. Men can stop their violent behaviour if they complete a perpetrator programme, and we should not disregard the possibility of successful reunion, free from violence.

Already a nuclear-free zone and presently a war-free zone, Latin America must take the opportunity to break the cycle of violence. Governments must take the next step to put an end to militarization of the region. The removal of all foreign military bases from the region, followed by peace treaties, are steps that can lead to a truly non-violent region. We have to imagine another world – one free of violence in the Americas.

Notes to Chapter 9

1 Associated Press in Colombo, 5 September 2016.
2 Dawn Paley, *Drug War Capitalism*, pp. 204-205.
3 Laura Chioda, *Stop the Violence in Latin America: A Look at Prevention from Cradle to Adulthood*. Overview booklet, World Bank, Washington DC, 2016.
4 Lewis, *The Growth of the Modern West Indies*, p. 93.
5 Lewis, *The Growth of the Modern West Indies*, p. 93.
6 *The Daily Observer*. "Caribbean Countries reaffirm commitment to UN 2030 Agenda for Sustainable Development", Mexico City, 30 April 2017.
7 Researchers Roberto Briceno-Leon of the Universidad Central de Venezuela, Andres Villaveles of the Universidad del Valle in Cali, Colombia and Alberto Concha-Eastman of University of North Carolina.
8 Andres Oppenheimer, "Latin AMERICA'S Time Bomb: the 'ninis'", *Stabroek News*, 26 January 2016.
9 Benjamin Widner, Manuel Reyes-Loya and Carl Enomoto of New Mexico State University, Las Cruces.
10 "Most Chicago Police accused of domestic violence go undisciplined". The ABC71 Team investigation by Chuck Goudie and Ross Weinder, Christine Tresssel, Barb Markoff, 17 February 2017.
11 Strauss, Geddy and Smith, *Physical Violence in American Families*, Transaction Publishers, 1990.
12 Peled, Einat, Peter G. Jaffe & Jeffery L. Edleson (eds), *Ending the Cycle of Violence: Community Responses to Children of Battered Women*, Thousand Oaks, California: Sage Publications, 1995.
13 "On-Screen Violence Damages Children As Much As Seeing It In Reality". Caribbean 360, 22 September 2016.
14 Paley, *Drug War Capitalism*, p. 51.
15 Paley, *Drug War Capitalism*, p. 170.

Chapter 10

DEFEATING DOMESTIC
VIOLENCE – MEN'S WORK

The region of the Americas is the most dangerous place to be a woman, or a man for that matter. In 2015 we killed more men and women here than were killed in the three wars raging in Iraq, Syria and Afghanistan combined. In the countries at war, it is mostly Americans doing the killing, or supplying the arms for the killings. We are heavily invested in the business of death and destruction worldwide, our neighbour to the north being the number-one arms supplier, with military bases in some 38 countries worldwide – more than any other country.

It is reasonable to believe that the levels of violence in the region today may have something to do with our history of violence. Let me refresh your memory. The region experienced indigenous wars long before Columbus arrived with his conquistadores, who unleashed a wave of genocidal wars on the natives. The subsequent conquest and colonization of the region soon led to wars of independence from European control. After these battles we then became embroiled in inter-regional wars for territory, resources and political influence. The USA emerged as a world power after defeating the British in their fight for independence. The civil war that soon followed claimed many more lives in the battle to resolve the contradictions of African enslavement. After civil war, it was not long before the USA sponsored some of the most brutal dictators of the 20th century in the region. In addition to the trauma of these wars, the region is blighted with the legacy of the brutality of indigenous and African slavery. As if we have not suffered enough, we now endure the US-inspired "drug war", with levels of brutality making even the dictatorial wars seem almost like a tea party.

American women have suffered immeasurably in all of these wars. The rape and brutalization of women during times of war is nothing new, as historically women have always been treated as spoils of war. But in the present-day undeclared war on women, the brutality has worsened to such a degree a new word has been coined to describe it "femicide"- women killed just because of their gender. It could get even worse for women in our region if men do not accept responsibility for the violence and take action to stop it. Men have done a lot of damage to women over the centuries and continue to so do; the truism "violence breeds violence" is nowhere more real than in the Americas. We have to bring a halt to this tide of violence urgently, or the violence engulfing us can only reach tsunami-like proportions.

For too long domestic violence has been viewed as a woman's issue and although it is understandable that women would want to take control of ending their oppression, men cannot be just bystanders while women are murdered every day by men in the region. Women have done a tremendous job of putting domestic violence on the political and social agenda and keeping it there; they have struggled against the odds and deserve complete recognition and respect for their efforts. It is crucial that women continue the fight for change, but men must also become seriously engaged in the battle to end domestic violence.

We have been engaged in fighting wars of greed, wreaked upon us by capitalist and imperialist systems, from the time of so-called "discovery". We cannot end the violence under a system of exploitation that thrives on its ability to divide and rule. Defeating neo-liberalism is a pre-requisite to a peaceful future in the region. No longer must our region and its peoples be seen as pawns of the rich and powerful; by giving people-first politics a chance, we create political space to end the conditions that breed violence.

Change is possible. There is nothing inherent in men that makes them killers; it is learned behaviour that can be unlearned. We can change the narrative. We all come into this world completely good, but things go wrong almost immediately for men. Socialization for violence begins in the cradle and continues to our grave. Our ancestors, because they had to constantly fight for their survival, passed on patterns of violent behaviour to future generations. Although not deliberately, they nevertheless have influenced the way we still think and behave, in our "machismo culture". We no longer live under the same conditions as our ancestors and there are measures we can and must take to end the passing on of violent patterns.

Each one stop one
Despite the harsh conditioning for violence we endure as boys, we have tried our best to be caring; the fact that it is still a minority of men responsible for the violence in the region is testimony to that. We can turn the tide even more in favour of non-violence by interrupting the violence of just one other man. Most perpetrators are not happy with the violence they do and with a little encouragement from you, they can stop the violent behaviour. We start with the men who are close to us: our brothers, friends, fathers, uncles, neighbours, cousins. Most perpetrators assume that all men, by their silence, agree with the violence they do to women. If you are able to challenge the men in your life to stop their violence, it will leave them in no doubt that you are against what they are doing; by listening to their experience of violence and giving useful information, you will help them stop their violence.

If you have decided to help a man in your life to stop their violence, the more information you have about domestic violence will make it easier for you to make a successful intervention. A useful place to start is be clear about what constitutes domestic violence. There are many definitions of domestic violence, some are broader than others but most make reference to the economic, sexual, psychological, emotional and physical abuse. This is one I use:

Domestic violence is any form of sexual, emotional, psychological, or financial abuse perpetrated inside or outside the home, on parents, children, men or women by a family member or someone with a history of intimate or close relationship with the family.

Most of us recognise abuse when we see it. When we see a friend or family member with unexplained bruises, or in a state of unhappiness, we recognise that something is not right. If we are able to have that conversation, they will talk about what is bothering them. It is natural for people when they are hurting to want to talk about it. Most of us would have listened to someone complain about some unhappy situation. If you are good at listening, without interrupting too many times, more people will want to tell you about their difficulties. This is what makes someone a good counsellor: they listen well and allow the person space to have feelings about whatever is causing distress. It is never about giving advice. You listen to them and help them think about solutions for themselves – giving information is helpful, and offering to be there for them is what works. You do your best with the information and caring you have for those you are trying to help. With a little training we can all become excellent counsellors. It involves working on your own difficulties, so that you are in better shape to help others. The more information you have about domestic violence the better you are in a position to help; it is hoped that the information given here will be useful in any intervention you decide to make. If there is a possibility of the perpetrator seeing a trained counsellor, recommending such action is useful. For most of us, we will have to do the best we can, with the situation we are presented with. Refraining from giving advice will generally not make the situation any worse, than it is. Doing nothing when a loved one is being abused should never be an option.

It is not acceptable that we sit on our hands as our mothers, sisters, aunts, cousins, colleagues, neighbours and girlfriends are forced to live with violence on a daily basis. This is not a call to put yourself in danger, and it is well worth remembering that violence only breeds more violence. There are many ways an intervention can be made without the use of violence. You are in the best position to think carefully about any situation you are presented with and come up with the best solution. Men are good at problem-solving and if we take responsibility for ending violence we will find the solutions. We face a serious challenge to our very civilised existence and it is in everyone's interest to end the violence. We all have a role to play, but some are better placed than others to take action.

Policemen

Some of the most important men who can make a difference to violence are our policemen. Often the first on the scene of domestic violence, they have a crucial role in having a positive outcome. I have often criticised the police for failing to take domestic violence seriously enough. Too many women have been killed despite making repeated attempts to get support from policemen. This must change or women will stop reporting domestic violence, leaving them susceptible to further violence. I have often pointed to research, showing the high incidence of domestic violence in the police force itself. Research has also shown that police men have often taken advantage of vulnerable women. These issues need to be addressed with appropriate sanctions and training to support change in the police force.

Being a policeman is one of the most challenging jobs in the region and low pay and poor training will not deliver the kind of force we deserve. It is not surprising that confidence in the police is lacking as police are daily accused and often convicted of corruption, in almost every country in the region. Corruption will not go away overnight, but individual policeman must make a decision to do the best they can to protect citizens from violence. A lot depends on their awareness of domestic violence and a commitment to do their job well. Many of the men I counselled at the Everyman Centre in London became advocates of ending domestic violence and often recounted their action in interrupting other men's violence. You too can interrupt violent behaviour; taking time to understand the root causes of domestic violence can make your intervention a positive one. You have a key role to play in ending the violence. The place to start is to look at "the man in the mirror" and ask a few questions. Are you doing enough to stop the violence? I have written a self-help book for perpetrators, so will not attempt too much here, but there are a few things worth mentioning:

Decision

If you have perpetrated violence, it is because you have learned that behaviour and with effort you can unlearn it. You can begin by simply making a "decision" to stop your violence and remind yourself every day of that "decision" to stop the violence. It helps if you apologise to the ones you hurt and make a promise to stop the violence. It will help you even more if you become an advocate of non-violence. Interrupting the violence of other men and taking a public stand against domestic violence will help you to stop, as we hate being hypocrites. Talking about your experience of violence will help you stop your violence. Taking a practical step like the "six-foot rule" will help keep your partner safe. You need to make an agreement with your partner to activate the six foot rule whenever it feels like a situation is getting out of control. Either of you can trigger the six foot rule. It basically means you do not get within six feet of each other, until calm is restored. It might be a good time to get a breath of fresh air and reflect on your actions. Most of the problem is caused by you, trying to "control" your partner – you have to examine this behaviour and talk about it. It is a learnt behaviour and you will have to go back to your child hood memories to understand how you learnt the behaviour and make a decision to stop it.

If you are one of the men who have not used violence, you are in a good position to help other men. Perpetrators believe that other men, by their silence, agree with the violence they do. Interrupting the violence of a brother, friend, neighbour or anyone for that matter will send a clear message. Listening to the perpetrator for a while and asserting that the use of violence is never justified, will make them think again. Giving good information is always helpful and it is hoped that the information presented here will be useful for you, when thinking about making an intervention.

Healing the hurts

Men who hurt people have mostly been "hurt" in the first place and not been allowed to heal from those hurts. One of the natural healing processes of the body is to cry when we are hurting; we do this spontaneously. When we get stopped from crying, as happens to most boys with "Come on, big boys don't cry", the healing is interrupted, the hurt stored up and often "acted out" on people close to us. To be in a better position to help other men, we have to start with healing ourselves. Talking about the hurts you endured as a child, or even just thinking about them will help, especially if you are able to connect with your feelings as you do. Accepting that you were "hurt" as a child will help you accept responsibility for the violence you do today. There can be no ending of domestic violence if men do not take responsibility for their actions. Men need support to change their behaviour and attitude; no amount of imprisonment alone will provide the kind of support they need to change. To make real progress with ending violence in the Americas we need break from the neo-liberal approach to ending violence to women. Their approach can be summed up in one sentence: remove the victim from the situation and imprison the perpetrator. Prioritising women's safety is crucial and some men will need to be locked up to protect women; but this is not the solution to ending domestic violence. Defeating domestic violence provides opportunity for awareness raising work with perpetrators; changing their attitude and behaviour will help transform society and this must be part of any strategy to ending domestic violence. Socialization for violence and sexism play key roles in domestic violence and Latino and black men have long been stereotyped as being violent and sexist. This portrayal must be challenged and changed just as much as the notion that "real men" are tough and strong.

Paulo Freire, the respected Brazilian educator, argues in *Pedagogy of the Oppressed* that only the oppressed can put an end to oppression: "This, then, is the great humanistic and historical task of the oppressed: to liberate themselves and their oppressors as well. The oppressors, who oppress, exploit and rape by virtue of their power, cannot find in this power the strength to liberate either the oppressed or themselves. Only power that springs from the weakness of the oppressed will be sufficiently strong to free both." Oppressive neoliberal societies can never provide the framework to end domestic violence.

Make no mistake, domestic violence is a political act, action that supports the subordination of women. Men have been coerced and encouraged to oppress women in support of patriarchal rule for so long, they do it without thinking. It has become part of our "macho culture". Patriarchal societies are inherently oppressive, with almost everyone experiencing some kind of oppression and in turn oppressing others. Oppression here means: *the one-way mistreatment of an individual or group by another group or individual, often with the collusion of the state.* Most of us when young have faced oppression perpetrated by adults and we are likely to face oppression again as elders, this time perpetrated by young ones. Most of us will experience multiple oppressions, such as class, race, religion, gender, sexual preference, size and a host of others in our lifetime. When men join women in their fight for liberation we are taking action to end the oppression of men. Raising awareness about the oppressive society we live in will help defeat it. Understanding the root cause of violent behaviour will help stop it.

The root causes of domestic violence

To win the battle against violence in the region we need to confront it with careful analysis and theory. Just as the failure of a doctor to correctly diagnose the condition affecting a patient can adversely affect their ability to recover; failure to understand the root cause of violent behaviour daily results in death and injury for many women. Feminists have long argued that the root cause of violence to women is patriarchal rule. Understanding how patriarchy works will help in defeating it. We know that it is men who mostly benefit from patriarchy, but not all men benefit in the same way; a small minority of men have become extremely wealthy and powerful through this oppressive system and it is in the interests of the majority of men to defeat this system.

Gerda Lerner in her book *The Creation of Patriarchy* argues that the first archaic states were "shaped and developed in the form of patriarchy,"[1] and were designed to subordinate women. That laws had to be enacted to punish men who did not collude with the oppression of women meant that many men refused to support the patriarchal state, she argues. Under Middle Assyrian laws, patriarchal rule gave men complete control over women's lives and they were legally permitted to do violence to women, including taking their lives. The state often assumed the role of perpetrator, as demonstrated by Lerner: "Mal*57 states that if flogging of a man's wife had been ordered "on the tablet", which means by law, it must be carried out in public. MAL *58

DEFEATING DOMESTIC VIOLENCE - MEN'S WORK

reinforces this: all legally inflicted punishments of wives, such as tearing out of the breasts and cutting off of nose or ears, must be carried out by an official."[2] These brutal acts changed gradually over time, but it was not so long ago in England, that a man could legally beat his wife with a stick, providing it was no fatter than his thumb, hence "the rule of thumb" as we know it in law today. It is only recently that some modern states have changed oppressive legislation but presently, some 20 countries still have laws in place supporting domestic violence. Activists point out that even when laws are enacted outlawing domestic violence, they are rarely given the support needed to make them effective.

Domestic violence is neither inevitable nor acceptable and the recent history of resistance is worth noting. Briefly put, political agitation during the late 19th century led to changes in both popular opinion and legislation regarding domestic violence, within the United Kingdom and the United States. In 1850, Tennessee became the first state in the USA to outlaw wife-beating. By the end of the 1870s, most US courts were against the right of husbands to physically discipline their wives. In 1878, the Matrimonial Causes Act made it possible for women in the UK to seek separations from abusive husbands. By the early 20th century, it was common for the police to intervene in cases of domestic violence in the USA, but with few arrests. This attitude still persists in some places today and it is not too long ago that "it's only a domestic" was the attitude of the British police, when called to a domestic incident.

Patriarchy is at the root of domestic violence and is alive and well today, mainly in three well established, powerful institutions, dominated by men and very supportive of each other. They comprise: the captains of capitalism, religious leaders and the military. Defeating them will be challenging, but being aware of their influence will help undermine their hold over us. Let us take a brief look at these institutions and how they influence our lives.

The military

Probably the most powerful institution in the world, the military is responsible for almost all the violent acts of wanton, wilful destruction committed worldwide. This is what a decorated

US war hero had to say: "War is a racket. It always has been. It is possibly the oldest easily the most profitable, surely the most vicious. It is the only one international in scope. It is the only one in which the profits are reckoned in dollars and the losses in lives."[3] War has been a disaster for men, but it also costs women dearly; often seen as the spoils of war, women have been routinely raped and brutalised by conquering armies of times past and present. All governments depend on the violence that men do, or are capable of doing, in times of war. We have lurched from one war to the next for centuries; and it would seem that those who benefit economically from wars, are determined that men will always be fighting. Only recently Britain warned its NATO allies to "meet the pledge to spend two per cent of national income on defence" as Trump had threatened to not come to their defence unless they "pay their bills" and "fulfil their obligations".[4] Since Trump took office he has ramped up the pressure for more spending and has committed the USA to some $52 billion on defence. The "mother of all bombs" dropped on Afghanistan did not come cheap, it cost some $11 million dollars, and signalled that there will be no let-up in the pressure to spend even more on arms. It bodes ill for the Gulf States that Donald Trump, on his first overseas visit as president, netted a "$350 billion arms deal, over 10 years with $110 billion that will take effect immediately" with Saudi Arabia.[5]

If there were no need for fighting wars, there would be no need for the socialization for violence. The stereotyping of men as "naturally" violent has been carefully nurtured for hundreds of years by those who benefit from men fighting wars. One of the earliest, enduring violent images is the cartoon depiction of "caveman", club in hand, dragging cave woman by her hair. This false representation of Neanderthals, despite evidence of his "essential gentleness",[6] has left many of us with the belief that caveman was violent to cave woman. Just as we have been led to believe that competition and aggression are necessary for our survival, we have been lied to about the true nature of men. Men's violent behaviour has more to do with socialisation than anything else. Only by dismantling the mighty, military industrial complex can men be liberated from a lifetime of violence.

Religion

Religion has for centuries preached women's subordination to men, often with the state's collusion. Patriarchs undermined the role of women in religions and slowly wrested control from them. We must face the fact that religion has not generally been kind to women; one only has to look back to the period in Europe when hundreds of thousands of women lost their lives to witch hunts. Although the first specific law against witchcraft was introduced under Henry VIII in 1542, the "last woman jailed for witchcraft in England was Scottish-born Helen Duncan, a medium arrested while holding a séance in 1944 and accused of betraying war secrets. She was prosecuted for fraud and witchcraft and served nine months in Holloway prison."[7]

Witch hunts were active in Europe at the period when Columbus set sail on his voyage of discovery of the New World. Many of the early settlers would have brought negative attitudes towards women with them. There is evidence that many of our indigenous ancestors intervened if a woman or child was being mistreated, before they were discouraged by the European invaders from doing so. In his diary, Le June recorded what transpired when two Captains were ordered by the Jesuits to imprison a young woman for "disobedience". As the Captains attempted to force her into a canoe.

> Some Pagan young men, observing this violence, of which the Savages have a horror, and which is more remote from their customs than heaven is from Earth, made use of threats, declaring that they would kill anyone who laid a hand on the woman. But the Captain and his people, who were Christians, boldly replied that there was nothing that they would not do or endure, in order to secure obedience to God. Such resolution silenced the infidels.[8]

These same religious attitudes to women persist to this day and contribute to the current epidemic of domestic violence in the region. There is nothing new about religion attempting to take control of women's bodies, often with support from the state. "In Europe forcing women to procreate had led to the imposition of capital punishment for contraception."[9] This same attitude, advocated by the religious right, is widespread in the Americas today, highlighted by the case in Chile where an 11-year-old became pregnant as a result of being raped by her step-father. "The case has caused controversy in the predominantly Roman Catholic country, one of seven in Latin America with an outright ban on abortion." The report continued: "in El Salvador, which also criminalises all abortions, a young woman whose life was at risk from her pregnancy and whose baby was medically incapable of surviving, was allowed to have an early Caesarean section to save her life, after the Supreme Court banned her from having a termination."[10] There can be no end to domestic violence while the state colludes with religion to exercise control over women's bodies. Religion, by advocating men's dominance over women in the family, promotes the conditions for the abuse of women. The "spare the rod and spoil the child" approach to parenting, as practised by many, sets us up for a future steeped in violence, and this must be challenged if we are to end the epidemic of domestic violence in the region.

Capitalism

At the root of most oppression is economic exploitation. The rapid rise of capitalism coincided with the discovery and colonisation of the Americas. Eric Williams in *Slavery and Capitalism* has argued that the wealth extracted from slave labour created the finance to fuel the industrial revolution, making Britain one of the richest countries in the world today. Capitalism benefits from treating women as less equal than men by paying them less than men for the same work. Feminists have long fought for equal pay for women and have often cited inequality as one of the main drivers of domestic violence. When women are treated as less by society, it is unsurprising that men act out feelings of superiority over women. When women are denied economic activity to support themselves and have to depend on men to survive, it creates dependency that can lead to resentment and violence from men. To treat women as less worthy than men and pay them less – or not at all, as in the case of their reproductive and caring roles – is oppressive. Putting no or little value on these roles is adding insult to injury.

It is no accident that men own most of the world's wealth. Women have historically been denied education and ownership of property and are still denied ownership of land and other assets in many parts of the world. If women are able to support themselves financially it leads to more equal relationships and at least puts them in a position to escape a violent relationship.

Silvia Federici in *Caliban and the Witch* has argued that "Capitalism was the counter revolution that destroyed the possibilities that had emerged from the anti-feudal struggle – possibilities that if realized, might have spared us the immense destruction of lives and the natural environment that has marked the advance of capitalist relations worldwide."[11] There can be no ending of violence under a system that thrives on inequality and that is bolstered by the mighty, industrial military complex, as one of its key economic drivers.

Even the World Bank acknowledges the damage caused by inequality, "It is now well-recognized that violence is not evenly spread across cities, but tends to concentrate in particular geographic areas. These 'hot spots,' or 'no-go zones,' tend to have several structural features in common, and these commonalities extend across countries. That is, violence generally concentrates in areas of strong economic disadvantage, social exclusion, and poverty".[12] Replacing capitalism with socialism in itself will not end violence, as the oppressive behaviours learnt under 500 years of capitalist rule are deeply ingrained and it will take dedicated, thoughtful action to change these attitudes and behaviours.

Domestic violence persists because of misinformation and manipulation perpetrated by the oppressive patriarchal society. One of the ways patriarchy has survived is by the use of myths – a common way of learning about the society we live in. Many of the myths propagated by the oppressive society are destructive to our development and harmful to others and must be debunked. Here are some of the myths about domestic violence:

Myth: "Women like it"

Too often it has been said that women stay with violent men because they like the violence. Often the assumption is, that if she has not run away from the violence, she must like it. This is not true, women want the violence to stop. Often women stay in violent relationships for all sorts of reasons including fear and economic ones.

Many women stay in a violent relationship because they fear for their lives. The threats often enough made – "I will kill you if you leave me" and "if I can't have you no one else will" – are not to be taken lightly, especially when backed up with the use of violence. The most dangerous time for a woman is when she attempts to leave a violent relationship. Too many lives have been lost at this point in a relationship not to take it very seriously. Police, safe houses and counselling for the victim, must be in place when any such move is being planned. Ideally counselling also for the perpetrator once the woman is out of harm's way.

Myth: Women "ask for it"

I have lost count of the number of times I have heard this said by perpetrators. The storyline is usually: "I told her not to do something" or maybe "I told her to do something and she did the opposite – she knows I will get angry so she must be provoking me." When women assert their right to act independently, it is seen as challenging behaviour by perpetrators. Often perpetrators use violence to regain control of a situation, then blame the victim for the violence. "See what you made me do?" will be familiar to both perpetrators and survivors. Women must not be treated as subservient then get blamed for the violence done to them – this is oppressive behaviour. Men must get it out of their heads that women "ask for" violence.

Myth: Women provoke it

Yet again, too often we hear people say "she must have done something wrong". The assumption made is that she, by her actions provoked the man to commit an act of violence. This is to absolve men of any responsibility for their actions. Muscles do not move of their own accord (except for the knee jerk or elbow tap, type of action,) as instructions for movement usually arise in the brain. The decision to hit comes from the perpetrator and no excuse should be accepted for this bad behaviour. If men are serious about stopping their violence this is the first step for them – accepting responsibility for their violence.

Myth: It's between husband and wife, or man and woman

The belief that a man has the right to do with his partner as he pleases is deeply held but simply wrong. This attitude allows domestic violence to continue and thrive in our communities. Domestic violence affects the whole community and the community has every right to be involved. It is costly to the state and it is just simply wrong. It violates a person's basic human right to live a life free from violence, to be happy, respected, loved and cherished. If it is your sister or mother being abused, do you just accept it, with the excuse "It is her husband or man"? Or do you hide behind the "she made her bed, she must lie in it" argument? I would not ask any man to do something he could not do, but it is for each of us to assess what we can and can't do to protect the women in our lives. Make no mistake, intervention always has risks; you will need to be aware of this at all times, if you decide to intervene. Intervention could be calling the police or just shouting "Stop it!" from a safe distance. When I made a decision that I would always intervene, I had to accept that I might get hurt in the process. I was confident I could take care of myself in most situations and, anyway, getting hurt was part of the price I was prepared to pay in challenging domestic violence. I have a choice in this. The reality was that for most of the times I intervened, in the streets or bars with strangers, there was no violence to me, and the perpetrator was often thankful for the intervention.

Myth: It is the alcohol

Most of the perpetrators I have counselled were not under the influence of any mind-altering substance at the time of their violence. For the men who were under the influence of alcohol at the time of abuse, it was clear that there were underlying issues existing before the violence. Often alcohol is used as an "enabler", something else to blame, rather than take responsibility for the violence. Addiction to mind-altering substances does not help, and perpetrators must get help with their addiction. Most of the difficulties perpetrators face can be remedied with the support of a trained counsellor.

Men's work

Working with perpetrators to end their violence is still a relatively new concept, with only a handful of countries providing a service for perpetrators. The countries that do provide a service often have different approaches to working with perpetrators. The work with perpetrators could be broadly divided into two approaches: (1) projects that provide individual counselling/therapy and group work and (2) those who only provide group-work with perpetrators. Government funded projects tend to be group work sessions only, with clients often court-mandated to attend. At the Everyman Centre in London, UK, we provided individual and group work counselling sessions for perpetrators, who usually self-referred; in practice, it was often the survivor saying "Get help with your violence or I am out of here" that prompted the call. We did three months' individual sessions followed by three months' group work.

At the first session I always gave an explanation of the counselling approach used and my "world view". Sharing this with perpetrators is important for raising awareness. Briefly, they were told that, from my perspective, we all come into the world as caring, loving intelligent, co-operative, creative human beings, and if treated with love and respect we would naturally develop into wonderful, intelligent, caring humans. Unfortunately, most of us get hurt very early on in life, with physical and emotional mistreatment, misinformation and often neglect, which causes us to behave badly on occasion. By talking and feeling about these bad experiences we can overcome them.

I demand openness and honesty from the perpetrators I work with. To encourage this, I share my experience of perpetrating domestic violence. Let me briefly recount that here. Some 35 years ago I decided to do something about domestic violence after I slapped my then wife of 10 years. I had promised myself I would never be one of those men whom I had seen abuse women. My dad had instilled in us boys that it was only cowards who hit women. I became very depressed after hitting my wife and eventually found a counsellor, who was able to help me.

I made a decision after several counselling sessions that I would always interrupt domestic violence if I saw it happening.

It did not take long for my resolve to be tested – I soon stumbled upon a scene in the streets of London. Woman on the pavement, with a man standing above her and a small crowd gathered. I recognized immediately what was happening and moved with some urgency to attend to the woman. I could see no obvious injury, but she was clearly terrified and pleaded with me not to let this man take her with him. He was angrily engaged with the crowd but was quick to inquire of me, "Who the fuck are you? Doctor or something?" when I stood up and announced to him that she was hurt and would not be going with him he nearly went ballistic. We were now eyeball to eyeball. "You trying to take my woman?" he challenged, "No! She is hurt and needs help!" I was ready to defend myself but fortunately he backed off when he saw I was not intimidated. During this encounter the police arrived and arrested him. I then learnt from the crowd that he had pulled a knife on them when they tried to intervene.

I was surprised how many times I had to intervene in the streets, at bus stops and in pubs, in a six-month period. The response to intervention could be unpredictable: I was thanked by one man, cussed by one woman, thanked by a few women, attacked by another man. Only once did I have to use force in an intervention. It had occurred to me that I could get hurt, but I was always aware of the risk and assessed every intervention I made. Not everyone can intervene in the same way; you can only do what you can. There were times I have, from a distance, shouted at the top of my lungs: "Stop it!" I was always aware that using violence to stop violence is never sending the right message.

After completing my counselling sessions, I joined a class to learn counselling skills, eventually becoming a teacher of co-counselling. When an opportunity to counsel perpetrators came, I took it with both hands. I joined the newly established Everyman Centre in Brixton, London, and went on to lead the first group-work session for perpetrators. I have since then counselled hundreds of men, led many groups for perpetrators and trained men to work with perpetrators internationally.

Although I have changed many lives for the better, as a domestic violence counsellor I realized that no matter how many men I successfully counselled to stop their violence, it would never be enough to make a significant difference to the one in three women abused worldwide. I took opportunity to train men as domestic violence counsellors. Working internationally made me realize that regardless of how many projects established, it still would never be enough. It occurred to me that for every man I helped in any one day, probably another 100,000 at least, somewhere in the world, were abusing women that very day. That thought bothered me. It prompted me to write a self-help book for perpetrators entitled *Pulling the Punches – Defeating Domestic Violence*.

Over the years it has become clearer to me, that it is only by political action that the abuse and murder of women, on a war like scale, could be ended. With more than 10,000 women killed in the Americas alone each year and millions abused, it is clear that only strong government action can call a halt to the violence. In the previous chapter I have outlined some of the actions governments must take to end this war on women. No amount of courts, prisons, laws on domestic violence, marches and demonstrations, domestic violence projects, refuges, help lines and police officers will stop the violence. The challenge is for all men to take responsibility for ending their violence and supporting other men to stop their violence.

Working with male perpetrators of domestic violence is men's work. Recently the UK government finally agreed to pilot a project for individual work with men,[13] something we were doing at the Everyman Centre some 20 years earlier, supported mainly by charities. With the announcement of the new project, I heard the same arguments about why men's work should not be funded, being aired – by the same women who attacked our work with perpetrators, some 25 years earlier.[14]

It is important, that we in the Americas do not adopt the neo-liberal approach to ending domestic violence. Building more refuges and giving longer prison sentences is a failed strategy and not the answer to ending domestic violence; recent research suggests domestic violence is on the increase since 2009 in the UK.[15] The neoliberal approach has failed women miserably. The figures of two women killed every week in the UK, has not changed for the last 40 years, despite the billions of dollars spent on domestic violence. It is not rocket science to notice that it makes sense to work with perpetrators to stop their violence; if not helped, a perpetrator usually goes on to abuse other women. Having said that, refuges and support for the survivors are absolutely necessary in the fight to end domestic violence – but provide no solution to ending the violence.

Men must take responsibility for ending domestic violence and it is important that men be seen to be challenging men on their violence to women. Support for men's projects will help to develop male counsellors opposed to the oppression of women. A lack of appreciation about men's oppression, often gets in the way of those opposed to men's projects. Men need safe spaces to develop theory and action to overcome their oppression, in the same way that women have been able to, in their safe spaces, develop theory and strategy to oppose their oppression. It is by the combined action of women and men that patriarchy will be defeated.

Men taking responsibility
We American men have a huge challenge on our hands: reversing our region from being the most violent to being the most peaceful. It is work of a lifetime; making it a life-style choice will help. We need spaces where men are seen to be taking responsibility for ending violence, spaces where men can develop expertise and theory to help men stop their violent behaviour; maybe you can help by setting up such a space. Support for projects counselling men to stop their violence is an important part of the strategy to end domestic violence. Imprisonment for domestic violence might change behaviour over time but it is unlikely to change attitude towards women. A radical, feminist group-work programme, to change attitude and behaviour of perpetrators will contribute to transforming society. Survivors often complained that the perpetrators lacked communication skills, so we introduced teaching basic counselling skills in the group-work sessions. Men took turns talking and listening to each other and provided feedback to the group. At the Everyman Centre, we developed a 12-week group-work programme for perpetrators, and these are some of the sessions we offered:

To accept responsibility for the violence is the first step in perpetrators' stopping their behaviour. Counsellors have to work at this, as perpetrators often try to minimize the violence they do. I have noticed that most of the violent men I have counselled had similar issues:

1. They had been hit as children.
2. They had sexist attitude and behaviour.
3. They had been socialized to be violent.
4. They had witnessed domestic violence.

Our programme was designed to raise their awareness and give them space to heal from their hurts. Our group-work session focused on a number of key issues, including:

Men's liberation
Men need liberation because we generally live miserable lives, die younger than women suffer more mental health and drug addictions. We overpopulate jails and the mental health system, we top the list in stress-related illnesses and early death, including suicides. Recent figures of a suicide every three days in British jails is truly scandalous.[16] We hurt people and are unhappy with ourselves and often numb our feelings with alcohol and other mind-altering substances.

It is ironic that the system of patriarchy, created by men, is at the heart of the oppression of men. The system cares little for most men and would see men lead unhappy lives from cradle to grave. Ending the oppression of men is key to ending violence. Let us be clear that men are not oppressed by women, but by the patriarchal society as a whole – through its institutions, customs and culture. Patriarchal society has consigned men to two main roles: provider and protector. Men are expected to continually fight wars and this leads to the systemic socialization for violence for boys. We are expected to kill or be killed in times of war, and giving up our lives for others is an unreasonable expectation. The role of provider is overburdening for men and leads many men to take their lives, when they feel they cannot fulfil this expectation.

The oppression of men starts at an early age. We are denied feelings with "come on big boys don't cry" and get called "sissy" and other derogatory names if we do; then we get blamed for not having feelings, as men. Crying is one of the natural healing process of the body when we are hurting, if we are denied this opportunity to heal, we often act out our distress on others.

The world has been affected by the myth that men are inherently violent – the history of war is cited, as though the majority of men go out searching for wars. It is a myth that we men love to fight. In medieval times men resisted going to war. Force was often used to get them to enlist, and when they did, they absconded in droves, especially after receiving payment to enlist. For example, in the Scottish campaign of 1300, the king ordered 16,000 recruits to be enlisted in June but by mid-July only 7,600 could be mustered and "this was the crest of the wave...by August little more than 3,000 remained."[17] This resulted in the king having to rely on outlaws and pardoned criminals to form an army.

Men who use violence have been socialised to believe that it is natural for men to do so. The socialization for violence, coupled with the sexism men learn, creates the conditions for domestic violence. The stereotyping of men as being violent accounts for much of the violent behaviour of men. We are expected to be tough and strong and the pressure to be so is relentless, from cradle to grave. Ending the oppression of men is crucial to ending violent behaviour.

Women's liberation
Sexism is basically the mistreatment of women because of their gender. At its extreme end it is called misogyny – and we have real problems with the extreme end in the Americas. "Femicide" – the killing of women – is on the sharp increase in the region and men must take a stand to stop it. Sexism is at the root of violence to women. It is learned behaviour that can be unlearned. Many of our male indigenous ancestors were not violent, or controlling of children and women. These were attitudes and behaviour introduced by Europeans, as demonstrated by the French Jesuits who complained that the indigenous Naskapi had no concept of

private property, of authority, of male superiority, and that they even refused to punish their children. The Jesuits worked at changing their attitude and behaviour, beginning by teaching them that "man is the master", that "in France women do not rule their husbands". Also encouraging the Naskapi men to "bring 'their' women to order.... they began to 'insinuate that women who were too independent and did not obey their husbands were creatures of the devil. When, angered by the men's attempts to subdue them, the Naskapi women ran away, the Jesuits persuaded the men to chase after their spouses, and threaten them with imprisonment."[18]

Our societies for centuries have been so completely saturated with sexism that none of us escape the conditioning. From the time we are born the first question asked is about our gender; this sets the conditioning in motion: "blue for a boy and pink for a girl". Boys will be handled more roughly and given hard toys like guns to play with, while girls get dolls and soft toys. A boy really doesn't care at this stage what he plays with, but should he go for the soft toy, he will be discouraged and perhaps made fun of. As he grows, he soon learns that by making friends with girls he risks being called "sissy", or such derogatory name, and could be beaten. He learns that friendship with girls must be with one goal in mind only. He has seen the images by now, of women's bodies being used to sell everything from cars to cat food. He will see the beauty pageants parading near-naked women on television, and he will likely even have seen porn images by the time he is two feet high. His ideas are forming, too, from hearing the sexist whistles, cat calls, honking of horns directed at women. The songs he listens to with "hoes and bitches" will further strengthen his sexist education, which is nearly complete by the time he is a teenager; for the rest of his life the conditioning will continue and intensify in our sexist culture. Our role as adults is to interrupt this sexist conditioning with positive portrayal of women.

Giving up addictions

For some men addictions play a role in their violence, this can be addiction to overwork leading to lack of quality time spent with loved ones leading to tension. It could be sex addiction, often attached to pornography, which creates problems with closeness. It could be the use of recreational drugs that could have a negative effect for some. Alcohol is one of the main drugs used in this way; counselling to help with these addictions are part of the group-work sessions.

Parenting to end violence

Prevention is always better than cure; we can and must take action to prevent our boys from becoming violent men. Not mistreating boys and teaching them to be non-sexist, while interrupting the socialization for violence, will make a huge difference to the violence sweeping the region.

Nearly all the perpetrators I have worked with had been hit as children. Those who faced extreme levels of mistreatment often perpetrated the worst acts of violence. It is hard to persuade parents who have been hit and claim that "it has done me no harm" to stop hitting their children, in turn. But many social scientists who have studied the use of violence for decades have come to the conclusion that violence breeds violence. If we are observant we will notice that children who are hit and mistreated tend to pass this mistreatment on to other children.

Many parents in the region still insist it is their right to beat their children and often do so severely. The World Health Organisation said that men who experienced domestic violence as children are three to four times more likely to perpetrate domestic violence as adults, than men who had not experienced domestic violence as children.

Parents on the whole are very controlling of children; a child who does not respond immediately to instruction is often hit. This is very damaging learning, and most men who abuse women display controlling behaviour. Almost always the excuse for the violence has been that she did not "do as she was told" – from how she dresses, whom she speaks to or not, how she wears her make-up, how she keeps the home, how she cooks, how she parents…. The list goes on. Non-violent parenting with less controlling behaviour of children is a key strategy in defeating domestic violence.

Some studies have shown that our indigenous male ancestors were not violent or over controlling of children or women. Eleanor

Leacock in her book *Myths of Male Dominance* relates from the diary of the French Jesuit missionary Father Paul Le June, who was working to Christianise the Montagnais-Naskapi (a Nomadic Indian nation in Canada) and who had spent the winter of 1663-64 with a Montagnais band in order to better study their culture. He complained "that the Naskapi had no conception of private property, of authority, of male superiority and they even refused to punish their children.[19] The Jesuits decided to change all that.... persuading the Naskapi to beat their children, believing that the "savages" excessive fondness for their offspring was the major obstacle to their Christianisation. Another Jesuit, Bartholomew Vimont, records the first instance when a young woman was publicly beaten, while one of the Christianised relatives gave a chilling lecture to the bystanders on the historic significance of the event: "This is the first punishment by beating we inflict on anyone of our Nation. We are resolved to continue it, if anyone among us should be disobedient."[20]

Interrupting the mistreatment of children is one of the key steps in ending domestic violence. Parents must understand that when they hit children, it teaches them that the use of violence is acceptable behaviour.

When children suffer neglect and abuse they are more likely to use violence as adults. If the state condones violence towards children in school and the home, it legitimises violence and gives licence to teachers and parents to be abusive. Jan Carew reflects on his school days, in his book *Potaro Dreams:* "the head teacher and his staff believed very fervently that sparing the rod, spoilt the child, and so all walked around with wild canes as if they were natural extensions of their arms. These wild canes with the curved handles to provide a better grip were imported from the Mother Country, along with other school supplies, as valuable 'teaching aids'. Their 'usefulness' could easily be seen in the prodigal way in which they were usually applied to the backs, buttocks, bare legs and open palms of students, and the speed with which these rods of chastisement were shredded."[21] Coincidentally, the author experienced the same levels of violence from teachers, at the same school Jan Carew attended, three generations on.

For too long we have tolerated violence to children in the belief that it will somehow make them better children. Research has clearly shown that the opposite is true. We have to debunk the myth of "spare the rod spoil the child" to defeat violence. We must socialize our children to reject violence as a way of life. Many parents believe that boys need to be able to fight to protect themselves and their families. This belief is what drives many parents to support the socialisation of boys for violence. Only by teaching children that it is wrong to use violence, will we have any chance of changing the "macho culture", so damaging of our lives in the region today. Creating a culture of non-violence will take at least a generation of concerted action by parents and care givers with the support of government. There is opportunity in the early years of a boy's life to shape a loving and caring adult male. We have to seize that window of opportunity as parents and care givers, if we are to change the macho culture we struggle to survive in. The notion that "real men" must be "tough and strong" has to be challenged continually – and from the cradle – if we are to change macho culture.

Love Class

Often the perpetrators I have counselled profess their love for the partners they have abused; some perpetrators have even attempted suicide after they have hurt their partners. Many are distraught at the thought at losing the one they profess to love – they would do anything to get them back. Sometimes that is the motivation for signing up for the perpetrator sessions to change their attitude and behaviour. I am left in no doubt that many of them are deeply distressed at the thought of losing their partners because of the violence – but I also know that many find it hard to lose control of anything. They are often extremely insecure and jealous of their partners.

Love class is to help them see that loving and violence are incompatible. Truly loving someone means you want the very best for them. Love is not controlling. The truly loving person does not hurt anyone or anything and this is especially true of self. Most perpetrators of violence have been badly mistreated as children and rarely experienced what real love is about.

Many of us did not grow up with good models of loving; we mistake possessiveness, jealousy, insecurity and sometimes mistreatment as expressions of love. We can learn to love, and love class is about exploring that learning in order to change attitude and behaviour.

Conclusion: Fighting terrorism in the home

The real "war on terror" needs to be fought in the home, where more lives are lost each year than all the lives lost in conflicts in the most war-torn regions of the world combined. The worldwide toll of avoidable loss of life to domestic violence is unacceptable and outrageous in modern society. According to Alicia Barcena, the executive secretary of the Economic Commission for Latin America and the Caribbean (ECLAC), "Reality today batters us with scandalous figures of sexist violence in Latin America and the Caribbean, where, on average, twelve women die daily just because they are women. We don't want to lose even one more woman. It is imperative that we put an end violence against women."[22]

It is highly unacceptable that a third of all women worldwide are being terrorised in their homes on a daily basis. There can be no talk of civilised society, while this situation is allowed to continue and worsen, as research indicates. This is not a problem for the so-called experts but for each and every one of us to solve. Domestic violence has a beginning and must have an ending. The sooner we get to the ending, the better for all. Your action may be the most important one in bringing about its demise. It is hoped that this book has helped empower you to take some action to end this blight on our society. For much too long society has turned a blind eye and a deaf ear to the pleas from victims of domestic violence. It is not good enough to ignore that suspect injury and unhappy face and remain silent about it. Our task, is not to wait for that plea for help, but to notice that someone needs a hand and offer it. We are sometimes uncomfortable about confronting wrongdoing. It is better to face embarrassment than to live with the knowledge that someone was getting seriously hurt but you failed to act when it was in your power to do something. Right now is the time to interrupt the violence; tomorrow will be too late for many women. Many perpetrators I have counselled have taken great pride in recounting stories of their interventions. You too can become such a person. We need ask why measures for ending domestic violence are not directed at the root causes of domestic violence. Is it because the changes required are too huge to contemplate? Imagine a world where governments prioritise ending the oppression of women, children and men at the centre of its priorities. The Americas are beginning to move in the direction of putting people before profits. We can show that another world is possible, a world where everyone is treated with love and respect – just as the Island Arawaks before us did.

Ending violence to women is the work of revolutionaries. We have to join the likes of Che Guevara, Sandino, José Martí, Ramón Freire Serrano, Simon Bolivar, Fidel Castro, Hugo Chavez, Maurice Bishop, Walter Rodney and many unsung others in fighting for a better society. They had a vision of a society free of exploitation and oppression. You can make the difference in turning our region into such a place, a place to be proud to belong to.

Let us begin the work – your country needs you more than ever to end the violence now.

Notes to Chapter 10

1   Lerner, *The Creation of Patriarchy*, p. 140.
2   Lerner, *The Creation of Patriarchy*, p. 117.
3   Smedley D. Butler, *War is a Racket*, Round Table Press, 1935.
4   Stephen Swinford and Harriet Alexander, "UK warns NATO over Trump", *The Telegraph*, 12 November 2016.
5   Javier E. David, "US-Saudi-Arabia seal weapons deal worth nearly $110 immediately, $350 billion over next ten years", CNBC, 20 May 2017.
6   Obituaries, Pearce Wright on Ashley Montagu, *Guardian*, 1 December 1999.
7   Maev Kennedy, "Witches' marks: public asked to seek ancient scratchings in buildings", *The Guardian*, 31 October 2016.
8   Eleanor Burke Leacock, *Myths of Male Dominance*, Chicago, Ill.: Haymarket Books, 1981, p. 54.
9   Silvia Federici, *Caliban and the Witch: Women, the body and primitive accumulation*, Autonomedia, revised edn 2014.
10 James Hider, "Chilean girl is refused abortion after stepfather rape", *The Times*, 13 July 2013.
11 Federici, *Caliban and the Witch*, p. 21.
12 April 2011, World Bank Report.
13 Damien Gayle, "Pilot scheme to target domestic abusers rather than victims", *The Guardian*, 17 February 2016.
14 Sandra Horley, "The new DV scheme that focuses on abusers not victims, is one of the worst ideas we have ever had", *The Independent*, 18 February 2016.
15 Damien Gayle, Research by Professor Sylvia Wally, Lancaster University. *The Guardian*, 17 February 2016.
16 Nicole Le Marie, "Suicide in Jail every 3 Days", *Metro*, 28 November 2016.
17 Bennett H.S. (1937), *Life on the English Manor. A study of Peasant Conditions*.11.50-1400, Cambridge: Cambridge University Press, 1967, pp. 123-25.
18 Federici, *Caliban and the Witch*, pp. 34-38.
20 Leacock, *Myths of Male Dominance*, pp. 54-55.
21 Jan Carew, *Potaro Dreams*, Hansib Publishers, p. 36.
22 "Delegates at Conference on women strongly condemns gender violence in the Caribbean", *Jamaica Observer*, 27 October 2016.

SELECTED BIBLIOGRAPHY

Hilary M. C. D. Beckles, *Britain's Black Debt*, University of the West Indies Press, 2013.

Diego Durán, *History of the Indies of New Spain*, Norman, OK: University of Oklahoma Press, 1994.

Silvia Federici, *Caliban and the Witch: Women, the Body and Primitive Accumulation*, Autonomedia, 2004.

Paolo Freire, *The Pedagogy of the Oppressed*, 1972.

Richard Hart, *Caribbean Workers Struggles*, London: Bogle-L'Ouverture Publications/Socialist History Society, 2012.

Richard Hart, *Occupation and Control: The British in Jamaica – 1660-1962*, Kingston, Jamaica: Arawak Publications, 2013.

Richard Hart, *Slaves Who Abolished Slavery Volume 1, Blacks in Bondage*, University of the West Indies Press, 1980.

Richard Hart, *Towards Decolonisation: Political, Labour and Economic Developments in Jamaica 1939–1945*. Canoe Press, University of the West Indies, 1999.

Peter Kornbluh, *Chile and the United States: Declassified Documents Relating to the Military Coup, September 11, 1973*.

Eleanor Burke Leacock, *Myths of Male Dominance*, Chicago, Ill.: Haymarket Books, 1981

Gerda Lerner, *The Creation of Patriarchy*, New York: Oxford University Press, 1986.

G. K. Lewis, *The Growth of the Modern West Indies,* London: MacGibbon & Kee, 1968.

W. F. McGowan, James G. Rose. David A. Granger (eds), *Themes in African-Guyanese History*, Hansib, 2009.

Henry Marsh, *Slavery and Race: The Story of Slavery and its Legacy for Today*, Canada: Douglas David & Charles Limited, 1974.

Dawn Paley, *Drug War Capitalism*, AK Press, 2014.

J. H. Parry, Philip Sherlock and Anthony Maingot, *A Short History of the West Indies*, Macmillan Caribbean, 4th edition 1987.

Einat Peled, Peter G. Jaffe and Jeffrey L. Edleson (eds), *Ending the Cycle of Violence: Community Responses to Children of Battered Women*, Thousand Oaks, California: Sage Publications, 1995.

Steven Pinker, *The Better Angels of our Nature: A History of Violence and Humanity,* Penguin, 2011.

Walter Rodney, *How Europe Underdeveloped Africa*, Bogle-L'Ouverture Publications, 1972.

Ivan Van Sertima, *They Came Before Columbus: The African Presence in Ancient America*, Random House, 1976.

Ivan Van Sertima, *Black Women in Antiquity* (Journal of African Civilizations), New Brunswick and London: Transaction Books, 1984.

Alvin O. Thompson, *The Berbice Revolt 1763-64*, Free Press, 1999.

D. A. G. Waddell, *British Honduras*, Oxford University Press, 1961.

D. J. R. Walker. *Columbus and the Golden World of the Island Arawaks*, Book Guild, 1992.

Eric Williams, Documents of West Indian History 1492-1655, PNM Publishing Co., 1963.

Eric Williams, *From Columbus to Castro: The History of the Caribbean from 1492 -1969*, London: Andre Deutsch, 1970.

INDEX